Beyond Moralism

BEYOND MORALISM

*A Contemporary View
of the Ten Commandments*

John Shelby Spong
Denise G. Haines

1817

Harper & Row, Publishers, San Francisco
Cambridge, Hagerstown, New York, Philadelphia, Washington
London, Mexico City, São Paulo, Singapore, Sydney

Unless otherwise noted, the Scripture quotations contained herein are from the Revised Standard Version of the Bible, copyrighted © 1946, 1952, and 1971, by the Division of Christian Education of the National Council of the Churches of Christ in the U.S.A. Used by permission. All rights reserved.

Some of the material in this volume was originally published in *The Living Commandments* by John Shelby Spong, © 1977 by The Seabury Press.

BEYOND MORALISM: A CONTEMPORARY VIEW OF THE TEN COMMANDMENTS. Copyright © 1986 by John Shelby Spong and Denise G. Haines. All rights reserved. Printed in the United States of America. No part of this book may be used or reproduced in any manner whatsoever without written permission except in the case of brief quotations embodied in critical articles and reviews. For information address Harper & Row, Publishers, Inc., 10 East 53rd Street, New York, NY 10022. Published simultaneously in Canada by Fitzhenry & Whiteside, Limited, Toronto.

ISBN: 0-86683-514-8

FIRST EDITION

86 87 88 89 90 MPC 10 9 8 7 6 5 4 3 2 1

To my parents

Doolie Griffith Spong (1907-   )
and
John Shelby Spong (1889-1943)

Who taught me my first lessons in life and who provided me with the capacity to love, the security to live, and the courage to be.

J.S.S.

To my parents

Elizabeth Van Kannel Richman Games (1911-1967)
and
Denbeigh Warren Games (1909-1967)

From whom I continue to draw love and courage through memory.

D.G.H.

The Ten Commandments

And God spoke all these words, saying,

"I am the LORD your God, who brought you out of the land of Egypt, out of the house of bondage.

"You shall have no other gods before me.

"You shall not make for yourself a graven image, or any likeness of anything that is in heaven above, or that is in the earth beneath, or that is in the water under the earth; you shall not bow down to them or serve them; for I the LORD your God am a jealous God, visiting the iniquity of the fathers upon the children to the third and the fourth generation of those who hate me, but showing steadfast love to thousands of those who love me and keep my commandments.

"You shall not take the name of the LORD your God in vain; for the LORD will not hold him guiltless who takes his name in vain.

"Remember the sabbath day, to keep it holy. Six days you shall labor, and do all your work; but the seventh day is a sabbath to the LORD your God; in it you shall not do any work, you, or your son, or your daughter, your manservant, or your maidservant, or your cattle, or the sojourner who is within your gates; for in six days the LORD made heaven and earth, the sea, and all that is in them, and rested the seventh day; therefore the LORD blessed the sabbath day and hallowed it.

"Honor your father and your mother, that your days may be long in the land which the LORD your God gives you.

"You shall not kill.

"You shall not commit adultery.

"You shall not steal.

"You shall not bear false witness against your neighbor.

"You shall not covet your neighbor's house; you shall not covet your neighbor's wife, or his manservant, or his maidservant, or his ox, or his ass, or anything that is your neighbor's."

Exodus 20:1-17

CONTENTS

PREFACE

This book is a new venture in writing for both of its authors. It is based upon an earlier book, *The Living Commandments,* that was published in 1977 as the work of a single author. The preparation, the study, and the perspective on life that generated its content was shaped by the experience of that man. He was an Episcopal priest who was elected to the office of bishop in the middle of the book's gestation. He was a child of the South and far more provincial than even he imagined. The original volume reflected a limited worldview, a relatively stable and static environment, and a strikingly male and moralistic prejudice. Nevertheless, within those bounds it was received as a fresh, liberal, and controversial treatment of some of the major ethical issues of the day. In spite of its limitations, the book circulated well and only in 1984 went out of print.

In the nine years since that book's publication the world has changed, and so has its original author. Living now in the eclectic marketplace of the metropolitan New York area, embracing the pluralism of an expanding consciousness in a rapidly shrinking world, and being confronted by old values that are dying and new values that are emerging, he has come to some new perspectives on Christian ethics for this contemporary era.

In the past decade, rapid change has affected public and private attitudes and lifestyles. Family patterns have continued to shift with the rising divorce rate and the delay in childbearing among young professionals. More than forty percent of the households in America are now single-parent or single-person households. Lengthened expectancy has put unexpected pressures on institutions that are unprepared for such tenured relationships: marriage, pension funds, Social Security, and medical facilities. Homosexuals have continued to come out of the closets into which the fears of the majority had assigned them. New strains of sexually transmitted diseases have brought heightened anxieties. National boundaries, which are important in helping people define themselves and establish their values, have become increasingly porous as oppressed people migrate in search of a better life. In most of the countries of the modern world, legalized abortion is more widely practiced than many had anticipated. In advanced societies new technology has created life-support systems that in turn have forced new legal definitions of clinical death and have raised new issues of biomedical ethics. Population explosions and environmental crises have presented us with pictures of starving populations. The roles of women continue to expand. This is symbolized in this country by a woman judge on the Supreme Court and a woman candidate for Vice President of the United States. Many observers believe the Episcopal Church will elect its first woman bishop by 1990. Religious institutions have shifted slowly but surely to the right and have hardened their positions on many issues, such as opposition to birth control, adherence to strict orthodoxy, and defense of various claims of infallibility in some form. The movement of the religious right has captured the attention of the media and has masked the ever-widening erosion of religious power and religious influence.

Obviously, a book that sought to address the ethical issues of our day from the perspective of the Judeo-Christian faith community would need to be revised, changed, and updated in such a world. Indeed, something close to a new book had to be envisioned.

But can a person who wrote a work years ago escape the bondage of his previous words to say anything new enough, fresh enough, or challenging enough to warrant another effort to address the same concerns in print? When the publisher suggested that possibility to the author, he made no immediate response.

Yes, the author had changed. He had published two volumes since *The Living Commandments* had first seen the light of day. He had grown older by almost a decade. He had adjusted to many moments of trauma, both personal and professional, that had brought a measure of patience and bent him if ever so slightly under the weight of age. But had he changed enough, or did he know enough, to undertake such a task?

At that point the author's life crossed the co-author's life in a significant way. The co-author was one of the early women priests of the Episcopal Church. The author, as her bishop, had ordained her to the priesthood in 1977. He had admired her abilities and her writing skills. In early adulthood she had been a musician. A career as wife and mother followed. At the midpoint of her life she had entered the General Theological Seminary in New York City with no conscious intention to be ordained, but simply, as she said, to satisfy a theological appetite that had been growing for some time. It was for her a life-changing decision. At some point in that process she crossed the Rubicon. She received her Master of Divinity degree in the spring of 1977, just about the time *The Living Commandments* made its appearance in the bookstores. She was ordained deacon and priest that year. Continuing her education, she was fully certified in 1981 by the American Association for Clinical Pastoral Education as a hospital chaplain supervisor trained to educate clergy in pastoral ministry. While in that process, she was called in 1979 to be priest in charge of a 600-member church—an unusual, perhaps unique, experience for a woman at that time. Her tenure at that church lasted for four years.

In 1983 she joined the staff of the Diocese of Newark as an archdeacon and thus became the highest-ranking woman priest in the ecclesiastical structures of the entire Anglican communion. At that point the lifelines of the author and the co-author crossed, and the genesis of this revision became possible.

If the book were to be revived and revised, it had to have a new focus. Why not the new focus of a co-author, one who would bring not only new insights and new knowledge but also the perspective of a woman? The idea was broached and accepted, and the work was begun.

We have in this volume labored to broaden the ethical perspective on the major issues of our day. We both live and write from within the faith community of the Christian church. We are both citizens and participants in the secular city of our day. Our style is to put time-honored principles into dialogue with ever-changing issues and behavior.

Revising an older book presents some technical problems for a co-authored version. What, for example, does one do with autobiographical material written in the first person? Some of it we have changed into third-person narration. Some of it we have left as is.

It is our conviction that the reader will discern and will understand. What happens when the authors do not agree? In those cases we first tried to talk it out and reach consensus. That in itself was a stimulating and enriching intellectual exercise. When that failed, we each wrote the sections about which we felt the strongest and then negotiated our ideas. Sometimes all that was required for acceptance was the softening of a word here or a phrase there. On other occasions it was not so easy. We can say, however, that each of us is now willing to stand behind the final version of this book though we are not equally enthusiastic about all of its parts.

Each of our perspectives and emphases is distinctly personal and seems to be conditioned significantly by gender experience. We hope that a greater measure of wholeness has emerged where only fragments of truth might have existed in the previous version. Neither of us would ever presume to say we speak for the totality of the Christian faith, or for the Christian church at large, or even for our own denomination or for our publisher. We are aware that many will disagree with some of our views, perhaps especially on such hotly debated issues as sexuality, abortion, capital punishment, and euthanasia. On these, as on all other issues, we speak only for ourselves, and those selves are white, Ango-Saxon, and middle class, but we hope we speak to the church and to the world. We are aware, however, that as a bishop and as an archdeacon we have been given positions of authority and leadership in the Church. Clearly, then, we speak for more than just ourselves; we claim to be a representative Christian man and woman. Our primary hope is that this volume will contribute to the debate produced when a living Christianity, flowing through its sons and daughters, speaks to the ethical issues of an ever-changing world.

We thank those who made not only the original book, but this revision, possible. Primary to that original volume was a group of people in Richmond, Virginia, where, through St. Paul's Episcopal Church in that city, the author received nurture and support. This group includes the bishop's wife, Joan Lydia Ketner Spong, Lucy Newton Boswell Negus, Carter Donnan McDowell, Eleanor Freed Evans, M.D., Frank Eakin, Ph.D., Cyane Hoare Lowden, Jo Anne Stoddard Palmore, and Jean Leonard LeRoy.

In Newark the original group included George Edward Rath, Beverly J. L. Anderson, and Martha Blacklock.

The new volume was assisted by a completely new community. The chief person to whom gratitude must go is Wanda Corwin Hollenbeck, the bishop's executive secretary, who placed these pages on our word processor and with marvelous patience allowed us to edit them again and again. Her competence and winsome personality place us both deeply in her debt. Elizabeth Jennings Stone, the archdeacon's secretary, also assisted in many ways, from typing to photocopying, and added her gracious good humor. The other members of the core staff—Christine Bridger Barney, John George Zinn, and James William Henry Sell—of the Diocese of Newark were enormously supportive of the project. We also thank our other co-workers at Cathedral House: Gail Deckenbach, Olga Hayes, Robert S. Lanterman, Margaret Allenspach, Barbara Lescota, Dorothy Lynch, and John H. Grady, for creating at 24 Rector Street such a loving and supportive atmosphere.

We express our thanks to Rabbi William Horn of the Summit Jewish Community Center for assisting us particularly on the concept of the Sabbath, and to Barbara B. Festa for her meticulous proofreading.

Finally, both of us are parents of children who now are all but grown. They have not been at home during the writing of this volume, but they are always part of who we are. To Ellen, Katharine, and Jaquelin Spong and to William, Andrew, and Elizabeth Haines go our special salute.

John Shelby Spong
Denise G. Haines
January 1986

Chapter 1

A PERSONAL BEGINNING

"The man who never alters his opinion is like standing water, and breeds reptiles of the mind."
—WILLIAM BLAKE

This is a book about ethics and rules, life and faith. It is written by two people who want to explore each of these categories.

Neither of us is a universal person. We are particular people with particular heritages and particular attitudes. We have been shaped by our environment and by our century. We speak with no wisdom beyond the experiences of our lives as they have interacted with our upbringing, education, and deepest commitments.

That one of us is a woman and the other a man means that our perspectives are often at variance, yet we have a mutuality in theological interest and method that has made a blending of our minds possible.

Both of us are Christians. We are convinced that God has entered human history uniquely and decisively in Jesus of Nazareth, but we are not wedded to any particular explanation as to how that great and mighty wonder actually came to pass. Above all else, we want to be theologically and experientially honest—honest about what we believe and how we live out that belief. We also want to be open and capable of moving into new conclusions when the living of life seems to push us in new directions.

Our rearing was dissimilar. One of us grew up in a relatively poor family in the South where the family upbringing was strict, moralistic, and deeply shaped by rigid Calvinistic attitudes. Ethical issues were seldom discussed in that home because there was "nothing to discuss." Every moral question seemed to have a clear and self-evident answer that left little, if any, room for debate. In that environment there were only two moral categories: right and wrong. The content of those two categories was assumed to be certain, and results of violating the moral code equally certain. If bad behavior managed to escape human notice, which was a rare occurrence, one was assured that nothing was hidden from

God's all-seeing eyes. If the scales of reward and punishment for good and bad behavior were not balanced here on earth, they would be balanced beyond the grave in the heavenly places or in the fiery pits of hell. When the code was breached, earthly instruction was given with a switch picked from a forsythia shrub. There was never much doubt that good and evil were clear, simple, and distinct categories.

There was great security in such an upbringing. But it also produced an unthinking and highly judgmental attitude. Insecurity or uncertainty was covered, in that era, with dogmatic pronouncements that made rigidity appear virtuous.

The other of us had a more gentle and genteel rearing in a border state. There was a higher level of culture and affluence and the added status of being the only child. Musical talent brought both acclaim and a stage presence. A broader community life produced an earlier experience of a pluralistic world, an appreciation for a wide variety of religious attitudes, and an ability to discern and respond to meanings beneath the level of rational forms or verbal constructs.

Some eight years separate us in age. It seems like very little, but when that span is placed upon the pages of history it makes some vital differences. The earliest memory of the older is the economic hardship of the depression, while the younger knew only the full employment of a war-time economy. When World War II ended in the birth of the atomic era, one of us was fourteen—able to comprehend and to fear. The other was six—with only a vague memory of blackouts, dirges of the Roosevelt funeral, the death of a test-pilot uncle, and silence around the dining table on a hot August night after Hiroshima's destruction.

When the Supreme Court case of Brown vs. The Board of Education outlawed segregation in the United States in 1954, one of us was on the verge of a ministerial career that would be spent substantially in that region of the country where the impact of the decision would be all-encompassing. He would live for twenty years with both the joy and the hope, as well as the scars, produced by that decision. The other was a junior in a high school that integrated twenty black students into her class of 300 and elected one of them student government president the following year. The class went on to integrate their state university.

Time, however, would change the focus of these two lives, as it always does. The feminist movement would affect the male in this author duet primarily through his daughters. It would be life-changing for the female. The male tended to pursue rational interests. He is a theological critic, a seeker after objective data, a driving debater inclined to the iconoclastic in his search for truth. The female is far more intuitive and open to truth from all directions. She is more inclusive, appreciating the mysterious places from which symbols arise and the truth to which symbols point.

We grew into our adulthoods along these different paths. Both of us finally found our deepest identity in the priesthood. For one of us the priesthood offered an external structure that ministered to his need for order and propelled him on a search for that ever-elusive promise of all religious systems—the gift of certainty. He never found it. Rather, he found an appreciation for and a joy in the reality of uncertainty and hence of insecurity—an absence that led to the integrity of being an honest seeker after the truth of God. He has come to love living in a world that seems to have mostly questions and few, if any, final answers.

For the other, priesthood offered a channel and a direction for creative living. She was far more willing to experiment and to take personal and existential risks. Her thought patterns organized data into a whole picture; she was not concerned if minor details were a bit discordant. Hers was a broader and less meticulous vision. She studied the motivations for religious points of view with far more interest than she studied the rightness or the wrongness of those discarnate religious outlooks. She is more interested in the life-and-death categories of good and evil than in the legal categories of right and wrong that bind us to traditions.

Those are brief descriptions of the people who have undertaken to revive and revise this volume. We think it essential that our readers have some sense of who we are and the direction from which we come, for the subject matter of this book is both personal and subjective.

We will attempt to escape the straitjacket of a moralistic approach that demands single solutions to complex questions. We are convinced that we must separate the content that informs ethical decisions from the practice of decision making—which frequently means choosing between alternatives of which none is perfect. We believe there are some clear and desirable standards of morality.

We are not convinced they are ever universally applicable in the exigencies of our human pilgrimage. There are few aspects of human behavior that we have not confronted in our combined forty-one years of rich pastoral experiences. Life has a curious and wonderful way of moving us beyond moralism and preconceived notions of propriety and into a quest for life-giving freedom that requires us to consider the limiting circumstances of every situation. We accept the pain and the joy of this freedom, the consequences of having to live with our imperfect choices. We believe that a code of human behavior such as the Ten Commandments, conceived more than 3,500 years ago, and replicated with almost universal adherence among human beings, must generally support the goodness of being free and alive, or it would not have prevailed. But if any code undermines the aspirations of our deepest humanity, then it is that humanity and not the moral code that must finally be served.

From this varied mixture of lives and background, interests, and commitments, we enter this study of the book of Exodus in general and of the Ten Commandments in particular. We want to affirm the truth that lies underneath this ancient code—a truth that has endured the test of time. But we also want to free that truth from its rigid, ancient context so that it might be freshly heard in the setting of our world and our century. We want to perceive the heart of the law as the creator of wholeness rather than as the moralistic arbiter of rightness.

A book is a very personal thing, a sharing, if you will, of what is valuable in the lives of the authors. We trust that this work will be received as such, and if some part of what is real to us makes contact with something that is real in the lives of our readers, then our purpose will be achieved.

Shalom.

Chapter 2

SINAI'S CALL: AWE AND WONDER

"The sacred is always addressing us through the world."
—MARTIN BUBER

In one suburban congregation of rather socially prominent, conservative Episcopalians in a small Southern city, the clergy and staff had received criticism for inadequate Bible content in the church-school program. The problems of the parish's teenagers were blamed on the church, whose staff was "no longer teaching the basics." At a lively social event one evening, a woman with a troubled adolescent daughter approached her minister, holding a drink that was obviously not her first of the evening. She began to lecture the pastor on the failure of the church to give proper instruction and moral guidance to the yonger generation. Her strongest and most self-evident point was that children no longer were required to memorize the Ten Commandments. The exasperated target of her complaints threw caution to the wind, and replied: "Madam, do you know the Ten Commandments?" "Of course," she responded, somewhat insulted by the question. "Name them!" he challenged. There was a cough, a sputter, an angry look. Finally she remembered adultery and murder! The conversation terminated rather abruptly. Her anger was not only at her failed recitation, but also at her failure to know how to have that acknowledged standard operate for good in her life.

Almost everyone has heard of the Ten Commandments. Some might even know that the familiar version of them is found in the book of Exodus. Countless numbers of people have considered these commandments a vital part of their religious heritage. In colonial times they were regularly posted on the church walls for the edification of the congregation that might be bored by the sermon. Many a Sunday-school pupil has committed them to memory. To many adults they are considered to be vastly important as a moral standard, even when memory of their specific content was dimmed. To join that sense of importance with content that is relevant for today is the purpose for which this book has been written.

These Commandments, as we will discover time and time again, harbor controversy, theological puzzles, and bewildering predicaments. To engage the meaning of the Commandments requires a commitment both to the integrity of the biblical context and to the integrity of the twentieth century. Contemporary moral issues are never decided on the whim of unexamined opinions, convictions, subjective attitudes, and fears. Nor can ancient codes dictate formula solutions to modern ethical conundrums. Being faithful to a religious heritage does not require thoughtless obedience to outdated or misguided ideas. Faithfulness requires the courage to ask different and difficult questions, to live in the tension of imperfect knowledge, to test the present against the faith story itself, and not to substitute commentary for primary revelation.

Faithfulness calls people into relationship with God, not into a fixed set of beliefs about God. From the bridge of faith it becomes possible to look back into the witness of the covenant people of the Hebrew scriptures and then to turn toward our society with the confidence that we remain connected by a common vision of a just and merciful world governed by divine laws. That hope and that reality begin with the account of Israel's sacred history.

The Commandments are mediated to Israel and the world, according to the Bible, in an unusual and mysterious episode described in Exodus 19. This chapter is filled with interpretive problems, for it is a collage of more than one tradition. Separating these traditions, however, and trying to uncover the original is difficult and perplexing. The story is told with many images, intimate details, and mysterious words. For the children of Israel this is the momentous birth of their nation. In this account the covenant is born and the national vocation as the people of God established.

We examine this climactic event by setting the scene and by entering into the emotions and sensations of these ancient people through imagination. The story begins:

It was the "third moon," says the Exodus narrative, some ninety days, after the deliverance from Egypt. This wandering Semitic band had entered the wilderness of Sinai, where they had set up camp in front of the mountain that was forever after to be a holy symbol of their life and of their tradition. Intuitively they knew that this mountain and their God, whom they sometimes named El Shaddai, God of the Mountain, were connected. They lived at a time when people believed that gods lived by streams, in trees, and on mountains. It had been a great surprise that their God was able to leave Egypt and travel with them. God's assumed presence in pillars of clouds and fire were manageable, but this eerie mountain was another matter. They waited at a distance while Moses alone dared to come near to the terrible holiness. Their fear increased as Moses made the first of three treks up the mountain to commune with God. On this journey, God said, "Turn right around and go back to tell the people this: You have seen what I did to the Egyptians. I bore you on eagle's wings, and I brought you to myself. Hearken to my voice. Keep my covenant. You shall be my people, my special possession, a kingdom of priests, a holy nation" (Exodus 19:3–6).

As Moses made his way down the mountain, no small chore for a man reputed to be in his eighties, he must have wondered about those eagles' wings. The last three months had been miserable. The people were hungry, tired, and unhappy about not knowing where they were going. He was forever suffering their grumblings and settling their quarrels. Morale had been low. Of course they had been just as bitter and complaining back in Egypt. They were an ungrateful bunch, yet God obviously had not given up on them, so Moses would not either. Back at camp, he summoned the elders to give them God's message. They seemed compliant in their response: "All that Yahweh has spoken, we will do."

They did not really know what they were promising. They had promised to be the covenant people, but no one understood quite what that meant. No one asked, "How does a holy nation of priests live?" Everything was vague, and there was a certain comfort in keeping it that way. It is easy to make promises that are general and impossible to monitor. We can quickly agree that it is good to love and bad to hate, and we can live happily with that undefined principle. Then comes the specific moment when love requires definition, when we have to ask, "Who is my neighbor?" The answer is "Everyone," including those people regarded as social, physical, or mental inferiors. Confronted by such unprejudiced inclusiveness, many feel their security shaken, and they retreat from principle. Occasionally their retreat reaches the near-comic level of the person who said, "The commandment to go love everybody is part of a communist plot to integrate my private club and bring about open housing."

Platitudes are easy, innocent, and comfortable. They deceive us into thinking we can be good without cost. In his first encounter with God on the mountain, Moses came down with an amorphous generalization: "You are to be a holy people." And Israel responded, "Lord, we will do it." Israel was still in the innocent-infancy stage of the covenant: "All that the Lord has spoken, we will do."

Moses trudged up the mountain a second time, taking their easy reply. God appeared not to know everything that had happened below. Moses had to run back and forth just to keep God informed.

"Moses," said God, "I will come to you in a thick cloud in public view, so that the people may hear when I speak with you, so that they will trust you always. Go back and tell everyone of my arrival. Spend today and tomorrow preparing, and I will be there on the third day where everyone can see. This is how you are to ready yourselves: Wash your clothes. Fence off the mountain and forbid anyone to touch it. Refrain from sex." "Do not go near a woman." is the way the command is given—a sure sign that we are in a patriarchal culture. The fertility cults and nature religions popular in that area would have incorporated sexual intercourse as a part of worship of the goddess. This command may have been a way of reminding the people that their God was not seasonal nor bound to the earth. Abstinence is also a way to prepare for an encounter that will demand a taut, alert mind and body—whether that encounter be with the Holy God or with a mighty enemy. A man dared not risk losing his virility or his concentration (Exodus 9:10–13).

For two days they prepared themselves carefully then waited apprehensively through the last long, silent night.

Dawn broke with peals of thunder and flashes of lightning. A dense cloud hovered over the mountain. Relentless blasts on the ceremonial horn, the shofar, reached an earsplitting crescendo as Moses led the trembling people toward the foot of Sinai, whose summit was enveloped in smoke. Looking up, they saw the Lord God coming down in fire. The whole mountain shook violently; the shofar pierced the dense, smoke-filled air. Bravely Moses spoke into the cacophony while the people stood awestruck. In a thunderous voice God called Moses once more to the top of the mountain.

When Moses arrived, God again ordered him to warn the people not to come nearer, not to touch that holy mountain for fear of death. Not even the priests, the designated holy people, were to approach that mountain unless they were first ceremonially sanctified and purified. It was as if God were afraid the divine holiness could not be controlled, now that it was unleashed; even God needed to be reassured that the safeguards required were still intact.

Moses responded with some impatience. "Lord, you have already told them not to come too near. They will obey." They were clearly too terrified to do otherwise. Unsatisfied, God ordered him to return and repeat the warning just in case there was any misunderstanding. God seemed to need to make sure that all would be well. God also asked Moses to make yet another ascent, this time with Aaron accompanying him. Moses did so, and when he finally reappeared at the foot of Mount Sinai, he read the law that was to be the covenant commitment of these terrified people.

In many ways the history of Israel begins at Sinai. It could be said that the first real chapter of the Hebrew scriptures, in terms of faith history, is Exodus 19. Before Sinai, before Exodus 19, the Hebrew people were merely an escaping band of slaves; but after Sinai they were a holy nation, a people of destiny, a nation of priests ordained to serve the world. They were a people identifiable in history by their covenant.

Only after Sinai did the people of Israel look back at Egypt and see the hand of God bringing them out of captivity and into this moment of covenant. Only then did they develop the folklore of their ancient heroes, Abraham, Isaac, Jacob, and Joseph—legends spun around a sacred history whose themes were designed to demonstrate that this slave people's ancestry was in fact not slave but noble, and to prove that this nomadic nation had a legitimate claim to the land they were dedicated to taking by military might.

Sinai is the fulcrum of Israel's history, and whatever preceded it is the remembered folklore that served to bring the Hebrew people to this galvanizing moment. After Sinai they began their self-conscious intentional life as the covenant people of God.

Also at this point a tension was felt that marked the historic life of Israel and that later marked the life of the Christian church. Indeed, this wrenching tension framed the entire story of the Bible. How could a people believe themselves chosen by God without also thinking themselves superior to all other people? Was Israel's call, or the Christian Church's call, a call to a life of rank and status, or was it a call to a life of service? Was the claim of chosenness arrogant, or humbling? Was the covenant open to all people, or was it closed to everyone but the elect?

Throughout biblical history this tension was never resolved. Theologies of universal salvation typically err on the side of cheap grace: admittance to the promised land or the kingdom without cost. "Out of humanitarian sentiment," said Dietrich Bonhoeffer, "we gave that which was holy to the scornful and unbelieving." Conversely, doctrines of divine election err on the side of an exclusivity that separates, fragments, and isolates the privileged from the rest of God's creation.

The pendulum continued to swing between the extremes of the dilemma until finally the image of exclusivity and privilege managed to prevail in Judaism and set the stage for rending apart the people of the covenant into a Jewish group and a Christian group.

A crucial time in the formation of Israel's identity as the chosen ones came at the end of the Babylonian captivity when, in the late sixth century before the common era (B.C.E.), the exiles returned to their homeland. Under the leadership of Nehemiah and Ezra they began to build an exclusive, narrowly righteous group to which there was no belonging without conforming to certain behavioral standards. This cultic attitude was challenged by the prophetic writings of Second Isaiah, who proclaimed that the role of the holy people of God was to bring life and love into the world even through their own suffering. Serving as "a light to lighten the gentiles" brought glory to Israel as light-bearer. But Second Isaiah's cry that the spirit of the law superseded the letter of the law was a lonely minority voice in the wilderness. The Nehemiah-Ezra ethic met the structure and status needs of a frail and insecure nation. That theological point of view thus became institutionalized in the precepts and worship of the established religion.

Post-exilic nationalism unfolded into the Judaism of the New Testament. The Pharisees were not a monolithic group. Many were outstanding citizens of their day, morally obedient people who were the pillars of society. These dedicated guardians and keepers of the law thought they served God faithfully. However, some of them also thought their piety and moral excellence gave them importance above anyone else. They called upon that moral goodness as a way of proving their superiority at the expense of those who fell short. Somehow, they failed to see the universal human need for love, acceptance, forgiveness, and community. It was this inflexibility and lovelessness that Jesus challenged, in much the same way that Second Isaiah confronted the priestly Ezra and Nehemiah. The battle still wages from generation to generation in both Judaism and Christianity.

Jesus abhorred the prevailing vision of the covenant as exclusive, self-fulfilling, judgmental, and self-aggrandizing. He issued an invitation to service and openness and defined discipleship as the vocation of giving life and love away. He denied exclusive claims in the name of all humankind by insisting that God removes the barriers that we erect against one another. The covenant, he maintained, has no boundaries of race, sex, or ethnic origin.

Christianity was born in this attitude of inclusive unity. "Come to me, all. . . ," said Jesus. Yet the Christian church has repeatedly made those same Pharisaic claims to exclusivity. Christians who profess to serve the inclusive power of the godly love that we see in Jesus the Christ have all too often corrupted that Christian calling by desiring instead superiority and status. Jesus said that the one served at table is greater than the one who serves. Yet the church developed a favored priesthood by reserving to the ordained the role of serving the people at the table of the Lord and by making such service the privileged bastion of priestly power. Having institutionalized the gospel, we have consigned it to the dustbins of the past where "moth and rust corrupt."

The paradox of any historical movement is that it must constellate around a structure and organization but that those things slow its forward movement and dissipate its energy. All institutions have a tendency toward corruption. Human structures set in concrete the very life-giving experiences we want to preserve, and thereby distort those experiences. From the start, Christians began to select the emotions and qualities that were the most susceptible to organization. They began to demand acquiescence to creeds and conformity in worship as prerequisites to membership. In the name of rigid conformity, Christians have battered one another in religious wars, in inquisitions, and in heresy trials. The God of love is never served by a rejecting community dedicated to the proposition that they are the only true believers, the only fit worshipers. The Jewish covenant makes the claim of chosenness. So does the Christians' covenant. But the call of the covenant to both is a call to be agents of the God of life and love. It is not a call to stand in judgment upon those regarded as less enlightened, less insightful, or less faithful to a particular manifestation of God's revelation. Sinai is the place where this tension between privilege and service first shook the equilibrium of the community, where chosenness was defined by obedience.

The last motif of the prelude to the Ten Commandments is the biblical concept of the otherness of God. When perceived as visiting, or even as living on a mountain, God appeared as an awesome, fearful, holy presence. In order to communicate the experience, the Hebrews presented the image of a volcano, an image of unrestrained power—smoke, thunder, lightning, and the shaking of the ground beneath their feet. These words used to describe holy presence evoked feelings, thoughts, and concepts of a sensory experience that connected with memories of compelling terror. The Hebrews were caught by a terrible awe. In their fear they wanted to flee, and in their yearning they wanted to be brought into the life of this God. They could not turn their eyes away. They were mesmerized.

When Moses walked from the people into the cloud, he was validated as God's special instrument. When he returned to the people, he was radiant with a transforming glory that was so bright he covered his face to protect the people from being blinded.

Within the aura of otherness, the awesome, awful, dangerous holiness of God, the law was given with solemnity, with divinity, and with a self-authenticating power. This was the context for the demands of covenant, the duties of every human being toward God and neighbor.

Symbols that transform and illuminate life can be as beautiful as butterflies, trees, sparkling wine, rushing streams, and fresh-baked bread or as vulgar and horrifying as a cross of execution, blood over a lintel, or the empty ovens of Auschwitz. We choose our symbols in any given time from ordinary life, from what is available for all to see. The power of a symbol to convert us from despair to hope, from uncaring disregard for suffering to resolute compassion, from survival mentality to unquenchable *joie de vivre*, can touch us only if we have the gift of second sight. The desert nomads chose their symbols, as we all do, from the natural and near at hand, not from the unreal and fantastic. The phenomena of erupting volcanoes, desert thunderstorms, and mountain mists were indigenous to the Sinai peninsula, but the second sight of these gifted and chosen people looked into the essence of their world and saw the pulsing, beating heart of the source of life with whom they were as one.

To these biblical people, God was a holy other who could be apprehended through the known world and who bound the holy people through the word and deed of covenant. That covenant made demands and brought judgment, set limits and called people into responsible freedom. Election by this holy God promised no special status, no prerogatives. It certainly did not promise health, wealth, and success. More often than not, chosen ones lead troubled lives. Prophets rarely die peaceably or even of old age. As one rabbi wryly said, "I'd love for somebody else to be the chosen people for just a generation." Election by this holy God to this covenant status is a call of this people to share God's work of redemption, to endure and enjoy the righteous demands of God, and to suffer the abuse of the world for the sake of justice. One does not enter that agreement lightly.

The Bible is quite emphatic that fear is a necessary part of the human covenant relationship with God. God and fear are not separated in scripture. The New Testament does not substitute a friendly or a permissive God for the fearful God of the mountain. The gospel presents us with the same holy love expressed from a cross lifted above the earth, which elicits a similar awe and wonder. The sentimental domesticated deity that marks popular religion comes out of a much later pious tradition. Biblical awe or fear, however, is not the fear felt by victims or hostages. It is, rather, the fear that comes from recogniziing that a holy claim is being made upon our lives, a claim on our behavior. It rises from a sense that a mystical power is acting upon us—a power that we can never control, tame, or manipulate. This is no pleasure ethic. There is no dichotomy between public and private behavior. This holy demand has consequences. It pierces our deepest commitments and our characters. Until we grasp this divine immediacy, so vividly portrayed in the prologue of the Ten Commandments, we cannot truly say we know the biblical God.

The glory and the holiness of the God of Mount Sinai was convincing evidence to the people of that day that there was a God who could deliver God's promises. Israel's response was obedience to those principles through which life, love, and the fullness of God's creation were to be finally achieved.

The covenant, God's gift of grace, is followed by the gift of law, which defines the holiness of those who are obedient.

Chapter 3

THE HISTORICAL CONTEXT

"We are not alone. The past is heavy with meaning; it fills solitude.
All of us must be aware of it."   —BAAL SHEM TOV

The Ten Commandments did not drop out of heaven in a
paranormal, miraculous way, Cecil B. deMille notwithstanding. That
movie mongul's 1952 extravaganza, entitled "The Ten Commandments," portrayed the giving of those laws in a graphic, fantastic
scene. As the dramatic moment arrived, God was pictured as a divine
drill or a magic laser beam. Moses held the two tablets of stone as the
fiery finger of God emblazoned them with the Ten Commandments in
perfect Hebrew. It was a memorable cartoon version of history.
Television's insatiable desire to rerun that movie each Lenten season
continues to set back the cause of biblical scholarship. Of course, that
is never the way ethical systems are born or cultural taboos formu-
lated, nor is that the way the Ten Commandments came into being.
God did not supernaturally write the Bible; God did not dictate the
Ten Commandments. Moses was not God's amanuensis. Only the
naivete of children and biblical literalists would confuse such a scene
with historical fact.

The Bible with its Ten Commandments came out of the living,
moving, worshiping life of the Hebrew nation. The brilliant insights
they captured are nevertheless limited by time and conditioned by
history. These interpretations of their life with God fail to make
contact with many of the realities of our day because the people of
biblical times could not, in their wildest imaginations, have envisioned the complexities of the modern world. Eighth-century B.C.E.
Hebrews, for example, could not embrace the contemporary medical
technology of respirators and dialysis machines that enables life to
continue after critical bodily functions have ceased. They could not
contemplate the entangled complications of trying to relate decisions
involving life-support systems to the commandment "You shall not

kill.'' When the Hebrews created laws to govern sexual behavior, they lived in a patriarchal polygamous society where marriage was usually consummated within one year of puberty—a society unlike ours, which has separated puberty from marriage by ten to fifteen years. Neither could the Hebrews appreciate or understand monogamy. Their ethical standards developed from cultural patterns that are radically different from ours. To literalize those standards is to bring forward that three-millennia-old way of life as well, an incompatible mixture.

Most people are not even aware that there are three versions of the Ten Commandments in the Hebrew scriptures. These versions reveal above all else that for a long time the law existed only in an oral form. Grasping that enormous time span presents us with a major difficulty in seeking a proper interpretation. Let us set the stage.

The events at Mount Sinai occurred, according to the best biblical scholarship, some time between 1400 and 1250 B.C.E. Yet the first written report of that law-giving encounter is in the Yahwist document, as the scholars have named it, which is the earliest of the four major written sources behind the Torah. The Yahwist document is generally dated around 950 B.C.E., and its account of the Ten Commandments is preserved in Exodus 34. Most people have never read this version. It has a highly cultic flavor. The last commandment in the Yahwist's list says, "You shall not boil a kid in its mother's milk." Few of us are even tempted to break that prohibition. The important issue here, however, is that a 300-year gap exists between the historic Moses and the first written record of the code of Moses. Though literate moderns trust the written word as more reliable than the spoken word, the memories of pre-literate peoples were trained to be highly retentive. Designated "historians" memorized vast quantities of the stories, poems, and oracles of their ethnic sagas. Just as today there are actors and singers who commit a library of plays and librettos to memory, and Moslems who can recite the entire Koran, so ancient peoples were skilled in memorization. Though nonliterate, they were educated.

Another 200 years would pass before the second written version of the Mosaic law came into being. The Jewish nation had split in 920 B.C.E. into a northern kingdom called Israel and a southern kingdom called Judah. Years of civil war and various foreign alliances followed before the northern kingdom was defeated by the Assyrians, and its people removed. With that nation's future so fragile, some unknown scribes gathered the fragments of its sacred history and escaped to Judah. This version of their history, known as the Elohist document, was in time merged with the Yahwist document in the south to produce one continuous sacred story. The Yahwist and Elohist narratives were to the Hebrews something of what the *Iliad* and the *Odyssey* were to the Greeks. This was Israel's defining story. It was in this Elohist account of Jewish history that the version of the Ten Commandments with which most of us are familiar achieved its first written form. This means that a gap of more than 500 years exists between the experience of Sinai and the writing down of the Ten Commandments in the version best known to us. Five hundred years between the time the tradition is supposed to have had its genesis and the time that tradition achieves written form is enough to create great anxiety among biblical literalists.

In the seventh century B.C.E., the book of Deuteronomy was discovered in the temple during the reign of Judah's King Josiah. It contained the third version of the decalogue, preserved for us in Chapter 5. As the name Deuteronomy implies, this "second giving of the law" was incorporated into the merged Yahwist and Elohist documents to produce an even wider narrative. This merged volume was the book of the sacred scriptures that the people of Judah took with them into the Babylonian captivity the southern kingdom endured through the sixth and fifth centuries B.C.E.

During that captivity a final massive editing of the Hebrew sacred story was undertaken by a group of people called the priestly writers. Misfortune frequently creates a yearning for the restablishment of ancient patterns and a desire to restore the pure forms of yesterday's style of worship. This desire was expressed in the editorial changes and extensive cultic additions that the priestly writers incorporated into their sacred texts.

The significant additions that are found today in the commandments regarding idolatry, the sabbath, and coveting come primarily from the pen of the priestly writers. So do the incentive clauses attached to the commandments regarding the name of God and the care of parents. All of this illustrates the fact that the Commandments as we know them do not achieve their final, written form until some 800 years after the wilderness experience at Mount Sinai. During those years the not-yet-solidified law shifted and grew, sometimes in oral form, sometimes in written, but always in response to the living experience of the people.

Ethics are the very stuff of life. Ethics promote the rules that a people devise to guarantee their survival and to enable them to live their common life in harmony. These rules rise from within the special and peculiar life circumstances of that people. They need to be pragmatic and practical, with function and purpose both for the community as a whole and for the individual. Ethical rules protect people from one another. When these rules achieve common consent, they infuse society with a dignity and a personal integrity. They imprint all who share in them with a divine stamp binding them into a tribal identity that is related to their tribal God. The code of law serves as a reminder that the image of God is expressed in their common life and that their ethical behavior is a part of their tribal definition. Only when a consensus is achieved is the code written down, and at that moment those standards and norms become the law. Soon thereafter they are proclaimed as the expression of the absolute will of God and are incorporated into the liturgy. The divine law, the inspired code, now governs human life. Finally, a people attach to their law a prologue that tells the story of how these rules were first received. That story almost always roots them, not in the common life of the people—that would be too ordinary—but in the authoritative divine will of their deity. The law becomes "revealed truth." This process has been repeated in countless civilizations and is very probably the path traveled by the Hebrew law as found in Exodus 19 and 20.

Beyond the history of the development of Israel's code, some general observations are worthy of note before we explore the content. Most of the Ten Commandments are couched in negative terms. As the decalogue is traditionally written, eight commandments are prohibitions. Only two are stated positively. Prohibitions set the boundaries on human behavior. They are designed to curb irresponsible and detrimental action. Negative prescriptions cannot force love of neighbor, but they can limit the expression of a will to hurt one's neighbor. Prescriptive law also assumes that human nature is not inclined to noble behavior. Only the commandment that enjoins the sabbath-day observance and the one that asks us to honor parents represent a call to affirmative action.

Even though the stylized liturgical form in which we now have the decalogue presents the Commandments as being given by the voice of God, after the second commandment the text of the narrative shifts grammatically from the first person to the third person. In commandments one and two, God says, "I am." After that, God is simply called "the Lord." Without exception, the one addressed by the commandment is the second person singular: as the older translations have it, "*Thou* shalt," "*Thou* shalt not." It is worth noting that this second-person form is rarely found in a legal series, then or now.

The number of the Commandments has never been consistent. Actually, there are only nine separate injunctions, not ten. The first commandment is divided in order to arrive at the sacred number ten. "You shall have no other gods" and "You shall not make for yourself a graven image" are parts of the same commandment. The Roman Catholic and Lutheran liturgies combined these two into one, as they were in the original construction, but then they split the tenth commandment to form dual injunctions against coveting, a device that served only to preserve the number ten. In Jewish commentaries, where the laws are broken into 613 separate injunctions, what we call the Ten Commandments constitutes 15, not 10, of that total. They are numbers 25 through 39 of the Torah. To the Jews, the first commandment is not the one about having no other gods. It is rather a statement of God's "being," which was implicitly a command to obey.

The biblical tradition about the two tablets of stone does not appear in the familiar version of the Ten Commandments in Exodus 20. The tablet tradition is attached to Exodus 34 as well as to the version in Deuteronomy 5. Nowhere is there a biblical suggestion as to how these commandments should be divided on the two tablets. Only later did there develop the tradition that lists one's duty toward God on the first tablet and one's duty toward neighbor on the second.

The substance of each commandment can be found elsewhere in the Pentateuch. Indeed, the decalogue seems to be only the barest distillation of the essence of the law, both cultic and ethical. One would suspect that the easily remembered ten precepts emerged into their familiar form as extrapolations from the larger corpus.

The Ten Commandments themselves contain neither sanctions nor specific punishments for violations. However, other places in the Hebrew scriptures prescribe the death penalty for such crimes as murder and adultery. In a narrative recorded in some texts of the Fourth

Gospel, Jesus intervenes when a woman caught in adultery is taken to the edge of the city to be stoned. The would-be stoners quote the law of Moses as their justification for requiring this death penalty.

The original shape of the Ten Commandments, once they reached a recognizable form distinct from the larger corpus of the law, was probably something like this:

1. I am Yahweh.
2. You shall have no other gods before me.
3. You shall not take the name of the Lord in vain.
4. Remember to keep holy the sabbath.
5. Honor your father and your mother.
6. You shall not kill.
7. You shall not commit adultery.
8. You shall not steal.
9. You shall not bear false witness.
10. You shall not covet.

The Commandments are brief and succinct. In their biblical form they are blunt, dogmatic, and straightforward, leaving little room for a post-Freudian emphasis on motivation. The number ten has both a mathematical and a symbolic significance. "Ten" lends itself easily to the memory aid of one for every finger and thumb. Such units are easy to teach and to learn. Numbers also express the essence of what they enumerate. The number ten is frequently associated with unity. In ancient Oriental thought it was known as the number for perfection. Pythagoras and Jerome both refer to ten as the perfect number. With its use in liturgy, the decalogue invests Hebrew worship with a moral perfection that leads to spiritual achievement connected to every other aspect of national life.

In the completed written form, the Ten Commandments are given a special place and a very special name. To the Hebrews they were the "ten words," the touchstone and foundation of the covenant. They have a finality. "These words spake Yahweh, and he spoke no more," assert the people. The ten words are enumerated in the books of Hosea and Jeremiah. They are mentioned in Psalms 50 and 81. They are honored in the scriptures as the first words that God spoke when God appeared on Mount Sinai. When first heard, says the narrative, they were invested with the aura of that mountain experience of incontrovertible holiness which allowed them to assume a place of preeminence in the life of the Hebrew nation.

Finally, the Ten Commandments reflect the essential character of God. God's mighty act of deliverance from Egypt called forth an immediate ethical response from God's people. For the Hebrew, worship and behavior were never separated. The forbidding tone of the Commandments sets the outer limits of the covenant. To transgress these limits would banish the offender from the established life of the covenant people. Overstepping these boundaries was not just a misdemeanor; it broke the very essence of the divine-human relationship.

The God of the covenant laid claim to the people of the covenant, inviting them to a new life and a new destiny. The crossing of the Sea of Reeds was an act of grace. Through no fault or merit of their own, the Hebrew people felt chosen. They were not a people, were slaves, the dregs of society, yet they were elected, delivered, and given value by God. That was the experience of grace. At Sinai those who knew the grace of God now responded in gratitude. The loved people of God now agreed to live in obedience to the one who had delivered them.

Chapter 4

I AM YAHWEH

"I live my life in growing orbits, which move out over things of the world. Perhaps I can never achieve the last, but that will be my attempt."

—RAINER MARIA RILKE

It all began with Abraham and Sarah when they left Mesopotamia and migrated to Canaan. We cannot know just what their home in Ur was like. There could have been famine, overcrowding, or plague. Or maybe Ur just was no longer a good place to raise a family. Perhaps there was crime in the streets, lack of respect in the young, and a general breakdown of moral values. Or perhaps there was a rigid class society that designated lifetime roles and made upward mobility impossible. Whatever the conditions, Ur was home, and people seldom leave home without a powerful reason. No matter how unsatisfying, home is familiar and therefore comfortable. We are loathe to tear ourselves away from the familiar, even familiar pain. Somehow Abraham became convinced that he should leave, and so he packed up everybody—wives, children, brothers, sisters, cousins, uncles, aunts, nephews, nieces, concubines, servants, animals, and hangers on—and took them off on a journey that has yet to end. A safe and peaceful home still eludes Abraham and Sarah's children a thousand times removed.

The significance of their migration was that in leaving Mesopotamia, they also left an array of gods—nature gods, household gods, worldly gods—to follow the one God who is the source of life, the creator of heaven and earth. Not only did Abraham's journey separate from a large heterogeneous population those who would become the covenant people, but it also set forth a new religious idea, the idea of one God who had authority over and who transcended the entire creation.

The God who is one arose from within a pluralistic culture that was also polytheistic. There were many gods in Ur who competed for popular favor, and everyone gave allegiance to more than one god simultaneously. All religions find their distinctive characteristics in relation to those of their neighboring religions. In every creed there is an implicit "I do not believe in. . . ." Doctrines and dogmas are constructed in affirmative terms that are illuminated against the rejected tenets of other belief systems. The early creedal statement of the nomad Hebrews that firmly located their religious beginnings in Abraham's monumental decision to leave home was "My father was a wandering Aramean." While this obviously described the kind of people who were eventually to call themselves "chosen," it also began to describe their God as one not bound by places, seasons, or material representations.

The mobility and the comprehensive reach of this new god-concept made it possible for people to sustain their faith while they were in transit. Their leaders were forever leaving home. Jacob fled to Padden-Aram after snatching Esau's birthright (Genesis 28); Joseph found himself in Egypt after he ran afoul of his brothers (Genesis 37); Moses escaped to Midian after killing an Egyptian guard (Exodus 2). Leaving home and going into a far country was often the prelude to an encounter with the one creator God in which God revealed more of the divine nature. When Moses encountered God in the burning bush in Midian and was commissioned to lead the Hebrews out of Egypt, he inquired, "If they ask me what [your] name is, what shall I tell them?" In other words, "To what god am I speaking?" Again the pluralistic and polytheistic dominant culture required Moses to make a sharp differentiation.

When God responded with the name "I Am," Moses knew that this was the God of Abraham and Sarah, the God who is self-named with a first person singular pronoun and a verb. This God is personal in relationship and dynamic in essence. To follow this God who neither forgot nor let the people go would mean that they would have to move yet again. They would have to leave Egypt, an unpleasant home, but home nonetheless, to go they knew not where. But there was still the promise of a God whose first relationship was to them and not to a tree or a rock or a city, and who would keep life moving. They would get unstuck from their slave life and minority status. They would be taken away from the competing influences of the local and limited gods. I

Am would personally preside over every facet of their destiny and would lead them to a new home.

When God spoke to Moses from the mountain to deliver the commandments, God began with a self-identifying word. It was not the god of the mountain who spoke; it was the one God who acted, not alone, but in relationship, and who now called for a response from the people through their acceptance of the divine law. The law given was as comprehensive as the divine nature and as relational as the divine person.

"I am Yahweh who brought you out of the land of Egypt and out of the house of bondage" was the first commandment according to the Jewish numbering system. Legalistic Western minds fail to recognize it as a law since it contains no directive for action. As a prologue to the Commandments, it summoned its hearers to acknowledge God's total claim upon their lives. God's "thou" had a stake in human decisions. That was the life-changing conclusion.

Here at the heart of the law, the God of the covenant was not "I am Yahweh, Lord of nature," as it was for the Mesopotamians and Canaanites, nor was it even "I am Yahweh, Lord of heaven and earth," as it was for Abraham and Sarah. Those limits were insufficient. They were distant, inimitable, impersonal. God could not be defined adequately by plan, attribute, or function. Reason and philosophical concept could not penetrate the divine nature. Relationship was central to the knowledge of God, so those to whom God related were part of the divine definition. The covenant was a mutual document. God called; God's people resounded. Each was bound to the other by the other. The specifically Hebrew observances that gave meaning to the events of life shaped all the biblical descriptions of this encounter. Those who live in history are formed by that history and understood themselves in terms of that history. They also define their God in relation to themselves. So the covenant asserted in this sacred tradition: "I am Yahweh, who acts in history. I act to free slaves and to bring justice. I act to give life. I am Yahweh, whose love embraces the lowly, the downtrodden, and the powerless. My love calls them into life. I am a partner in every human destiny. If you are to know me or discern my presence, you must enter life deeply, fully, and richly, for life is where I am found. I love because that is my nature, not because you deserve or merit such love. I act in love so that you might respond in love. This willful love leads to the promised land, a land of blessing and fulfillment."

Obedience in the Hebrew scriptures was not a duty; it was a response of a grateful recipient to the infinite love of Yahweh. The covenant people were not called to keep the Commandments in order to win the love of their God. They were invited to keep the Commandments because God had already loved them. Covenant ethical demands were the ethics of thanksgiving. The people of the covenant kept the Commandments because they, like lovers, yearned to incline themselves to the source of love, to this infinite, loving, graceful God.

Their acceptance of Yahweh as the God who was not absent from any aspect of life brought about a vision of history in which every event proceeded from the mind of God. Each catastrophe was retribution against a sinful nation who had strayed from the path; every time of prosperity was a gift from God. The Assyrians and Babylonians were understood to be agents of God, whose threat called the people of God back into covenant relationship. The Persian military leader Cyrus, as an instrument of deliverance from exile, was called messiah, the anointed of God. It did not matter that Cyrus was not a member of the covenant community. He was nevertheless under the rule of the one God whether or not he knew it or acknowledged it. Living in the midst of history prevents perspective, so it became the duty of the prophets to help the people evaluate current events. It was all too easy to mistake peace and prosperity, at the expense of the poor, for proof of God's favor. Amos put the lie to that falsehood. It was also easy to lose heart when threatened by invading armies, to fear that God had abandoned the people, and to revert to old pagan bargaining practices such as sacrificing the king's children in order to buy God's favor. Isaiah had more than a few words about those cowardly tactics. The name Yahweh turned the Hebrews to a way of worship and a way of life that were inseparable. This ethical monotheism caught up in a single name gathered and unified the whole of life.

Jesus not only lived within that Jewish tradition of relationship to a personal God; he also took it a step farther by calling God "Abba" or "Father." Not only did God have a personal relationship with a historical people, he thought, but God was related personally and individually to each man and woman as well. The relationship of Jesus with God was so loving and so intimate that the early church came to see Jesus as inseparable from the creator Father. "Jesus is the Christ, the messiah" became the early ecstatic cry of faith. Jesus was anointed and chosen to act in history in a decisive and unique way to lead all people into relationship with the one God. So the gospel writers could have Jesus say, "No one knows the Father except the Son" (Luke 10:22). "No one comes to the Father but me" (John 14:6). In time, led by a continuing experience, the authors of the Christian scriptures understood Jesus as the complete revelation of God. To know Jesus the Christ was, they believed, to know God fully and completely. So they wrote their understanding of what Jesus said: "I and the Father are One."

The church's experience of Jesus of Nazareth as the messiah re-formed, re-directed, and expanded Christians' understanding of Judaism's God. The church renamed Yahweh, Holy Trinity: Father, Son, and Spirit. Within the larger church, different groups emphasized different aspects of the Trinity. Some became theocentric, some Christocentric. Christocentric Christians were, and are, the most exclusive and define themselves and God in opposition to other religions. The more isolated they are from the culture, the more narrowly Christocentric Christians define the nature of God and the witness of God's self-revelation. Christ is not an avatar, one of many incarnations of the one God to be honored alongside Buddha, for example. Jesus the Christ is for them the one definitive and encompassing incarnation who is total and complete. There is no other valid revelation.

Conservative Christocentrism believes that the world must be converted to this specific Christ as the only means of achieving salvation. These Christians are not interested in knowing about other religions or in exploring the possibility that other religions may have heard other names of God that are different from theirs and that reveal more of the divine nature than a single personality or historical stream could experience or comprehend. Conservative Christians who know the name of Jesus and disallow all others, or who even disallow other interpretations of the Jesus name, do not value those human beings who are non-Christian yet lead godly lives.

By elevating Christ beyond the historic person of Jesus to a holy principle that operates in human life whether that name is confessed or not, liberal Christocentric Christians are open to non-confessing people who act in love and humility. Nevertheless, with them the particular incarnation of Jesus the Christ remains the single historical event against which all other incarnations must be measured for consistency.

Theocentric Christians are able to be inclusive when the Holy Spirit is the arm of the Trinity that is emphasized. The God present in all creation, who is not limited by narrow definitions and particular historical experiences, is a God who knits the diverse people of this earth together. However, such a generous theology runs the risk of pantheism, believing in a God present in all things who is available by immanence and who has lost transcendence, an aspect of God that has ever been part of reasoned theological discourse. Doctrines of the Holy Spirit rely heavily on personal relationships and personal experiences of God and err when cut off from the flow of history that regulates and protects the tradition.

As Christians in today's world, we still listen for the name of God to be spoken. God's self-revelation through God's name will have an inner consistency with the names heard throughout history by those who have known and confessed that there is one name to which every knee shall bend and every head shall bow. Just as the name "I Am" was given in dialogue, so that name continues to be given and heard in dialogue. With whom shall we have this dialogue? If we speak only to like-minded people, those who share our vocabularies and who know the same names and give the same meaning to those names, we will be spared the awful thought that we do not have an exclusive claim on the truth of the one God. If we can come to know our own mental and historical limitations, we are freed to be in dialogue with others who have different experiences of God and of life. To discover that God is more than we thought, more than we know, does not mean that our constructs are either wrong or necessarily inadequate. It does mean that God is truly transcendent as well as immanent. God is related to creation in wonderfully personal, intimate ways, but God is also unlimited in the ways in which the divine spirit becomes incarnate.

If we have the courage to enter into serious dialogue with people outside our own covenant group, primary among those with whom we would want to have conversation are members of other religions—such as Hindus, Moslems, Buddhists, and Jews—and, perhaps uniquely in our day, contemporary scientists, especially physicists.

Dialogue with other religions should not threaten either our creeds or our cherished beliefs. Serious and respectful dialogue with other faith traditions does not water down faith, as some fear. Rather, it gives opportunity to go deeper into the heart of one's own tradition. We seldom learn from those who share our own points of view; we usually learn in dialogue with those who differ, who see it another way, who have heard the name of God spoken in another accent. It is not necessary to incorporate the other tradition into our own but only to come to the wondrous knowledge that God is more than we think and more than we know. Unity does not demand consensus. It demands the willingness to accept the idea that God is able to gather all people into the relationship of a single human family that embraces wide diversity and particularity in the process.

Theology has been in dialogue with science ever since the two disciplines split. When theology lost its position as the "queen of the sciences" during the medieval period, it found itself in tension with secular science. As long-held God-concepts were challenged, the church entered the fray when the Copernican and Ptolemaic astronomical systems competed. Ptolemy had placed the earth at the center of the universe; Copernicus now insisted the sun was central. The church came down on the side of tradition, condemning Copernicus for his "heresy."

In the church's defense it needs to be pointed out that the church as an institution did follow the conservative route of all institutions by opting for self-preservation at the expense of new truth. But the church also insisted that there is no absolute truth except God. The church was unwilling to allow the new Copernican system, or any other system, to be in a position of absolute authority. The church was right. Our sun is not the center of the universe; it is merely the center of the tiny solar system in which we live. Much of the present conservative disapproval of Darwinism within the church falls into the same theological mode. Though conservative Christians err by insisting on the scientific accuracy of one of the biblical creation stories (of which there are at least five), they are right to insist that Darwin's model of evolution not be given a divine imprimatur or its secular equivalent, a status which prevents that model from being challenged or even seriously discussed once it becomes commonly accepted as absolute truth.

In this century, quantum physicists are proposing theories that are as revolutionary to thought as the fifteenth-century astrological debates were in their time. Sir Isaac Newton's mechanistic universe, which he conceived as a machine with all parts working in response to natural and predictable laws, has been challenged. The immutable laws of cause and effect that replaced immutable divine attributes of a personal God, and that divided life into religious and secular categories, are themselves being replaced by a new physical system. Quantum physicists, exploring the properties of physical life, are discovering relationships of time, space, and matter that lead them to talk about the universe and its components as a pulsating organism rather than as a machine. They speculate that the two irreducible characteristics of the universe are that everything is related to everything else and that everything is in constant motion. It is fascinating to remember that the name of Yahweh was a description of a god whose primary attributes were relational and dynamic.

Further exploration into the new physics may lead to the proposition that the dynamic quality of all matter is at least akin to the quality that religious people call spirit. Mystics and poets have not separated animate life from what is perhaps only apparently inanimate. They rather have glimpsed a unity that contemporary physics increasingly affirms. Second Isaiah's dream that one day the trees shall clap their hands may be closer than we realize as we come to know ourselves joined with the one God who is truly God of all.

Chapter 5

NO OTHER GODS

> "God is indeed a jealous God.
> He cannot bear to see
> that we had rather not with him
> but with each other play."
>
> —EMILY DICKINSON

A college dormitory bull session once settled into a discussion on the Ten Commandments. The peculiar twist of this discussion, however, was neither the listing nor the meaning of this ancient moral code. It was an attempt to see if the participants could discover any commandment that some member of that group had not broken. Some of them were veterans of an armed conflict; they were certain they had killed. Others bragged about their sexual conquests, their profanity, their successful episodes of stealing, their ability to bend the truth, to enjoy their secret desires, to disregard the sabbath and anything else that was holy. Finally one of them, doubtless a graduate of Sunday school memory work, shouted exultantly, "I've never made a graven image!" The group broke into a spontaneous applause. They had found their answer. At the bar of judgment regarding the making of graven images they were as innocent as lambs, as pure as the driven snow.

Little did they know!

A long-time church member once observed, "There is a God-shaped hole in every human life." Only God can fill that hole. When anything other than God is inserted into that unique place, the result is a distortion of that life. This was but a modern version of Augustine's confession, "You have made us for yourself alone, O God, and our hearts are restless until they find their rest in you." These two quotations move us into an understanding of the nature of idolatry.

The commandment reads: "You shall have no other gods before me. You shall not make for yourself a graven image, or any likeness of anything that is in heaven above, or that is, in the earth beneath, or that is in the water under the earth; you shall not bow down to them or serve them. For I the LORD your God am a jealous God, visiting the iniquity of the fathers upon the children to the third and fourth generation of those who hate me, but showing steadfast love to thousands of those who love me and keep my commandments."

The language is premodern, archaic, and sexist. Yet the meaning is profound, life-oriented, and futuristic. The world is learning even today—sometimes in joy, sometimes in pain—the meaning of the oneness and otherness of God and its immediate corollary: the oneness and sacredness of human life.

Paul Tillich, a brilliant twentieth-century theologian, defined God as whatever is a person's ultimate concern. God is that which elicits our deepest feelings and our singular allegiance, he said. If this Tillichian definition is accepted, there are no atheists. Every life has an ultimate concern, which means that every life has a god. The question is not, is there a god? but what kind of god does a particular life serve? What is the nature of one's ultimate concern? Does that concern free, or enslave? Does it expand life, or shrink it? Does it open, or close, the believer to life's deepest dimension? The object of any worship is whatever the worshiper makes the ruling value, the worthy object of daily existence. Viewed this way, modern men and women are no less polytheistic now than in the days when the Ten Commandments were being formalized. The objects of the heart's devotion take the form of the ordinary, not the numinous, the natural, or the supernatural.

Indeed, our prosaic idols and lesser gods might be all the more insidious because we consort with them unaware of the powerful bond being established through habit and addiction. Who can avoid contact with money, sex, beauty, food, or people? Any of these can be placed at the center of value. Not always are such lesser gods consciously chosen. Often we cannot even articulate our ultimate concerns.

Moral theologian H. Richard Niebuhr carries Tillich's proposition one step further. Not only do we as a people practice cultural polytheism, he suggests, but we practice serial polytheism within our own individual lives as well. The problem of life is not a problem of faith, for we cannot live without faith. Faith in some form saves us from the terror of autonomous isolation. We cannot exist apart from a supporting environment. The human capacity to confront the specter of self-reliant loneliness is the definition that Søren Kierkegaard gives to his concept "angst," an apprehension of dread that breeds neurosis and psychosis.

Neurotics glimpse the awful truth of finitude and alter their thinking and behavior in ways that reduce anxiety but that rely on belief in a false reality. Psychotics locate that false reality within themselves. They act out autonomy by living in a closed system known only to themselves and unrelated to any person or system exterior to themselves.

Those of us whose mental health falls into the category of normal (though many would argue that such categories are scaled with neurotic assumptions, for all of us are neurotic to some extent) make the necessary leap of faith. Fleeting glimpses of the void, the nothingness, the meaningless of life break through the bulwarks of the mind during times of crisis. Then we ask questions of faith. What does my life honor? Where is my security? Where is my faith? What threatens me? The gods who claim our allegiance are the ones in whom we invest what is most precious: time, money, love, even hate. They are graven images.

Throughout the course of life, our treasures and our hearts turn to various gods as faith attachments rise and fall on the tides of angst. These lesser gods never keep their promises to provide all that is necessary to life and salvation, and so they always fail us. Niebuhr calls this "the twilight of the gods," the fading light by which we could once see clearly but which finally disillusions.

A god who is trustworthy, whose light never fails, who is not subject to the vagaries of human existence and who is not in competition with other gods is the one God in whom there is unity. We long for integration, but polytheism cannot give it to us, for competing gods do not live in harmony with one another. Under the rule of these gods we work toward divergent goals simultaneously or follow separate standards of moral behavior that result in deep internal splits that leave our psyches mortally wounded.

When the god in whom we place our faith with assurance is one God, then our lives will reflect one standard, one value, one truth, and one love that is ultimate. That, finally, will result in one human family, not a family where everyone looks alike, acts alike, or understands truth in the same way, but one family drawn into unity by the worship of the one true God.

If God is one, then God's unity knits all of life into that single will. The law must be consistent, the same for friends and opponents alike. There cannot be beneficial rules of conduct within families without corresponding rules for interaction with strangers. There cannot be one code for citizens and another for aliens. If the God of life is one, that oneness will be so self-evident in all of creation that we see every person as holy, as worthy of care and respect. We then assume the egalitarian stance of people who will appear together before divine judgment. If God is one, no one is a slave. If God is one, there must be no prejudice and no bigotry, for every act of discrimination, whether economic, political, or social, reveals us as people who cannot tolerate fissures in the protective enclosures of a mind in which subjective preference is confused with divine decree and natural order. Every act of discrimination resonates with dissonance against the harmonic patterns that play in and around human life. Such discordant behavior is soul-splitting and leads in its extreme manifestations to a schizophrenic alienation in which all decisions are made with reference to the alone self's survival. With such a lonely and unconnected self, the many gods who offer peace at the expense of justice, self-satisfaction at the expense of mercy, autonomy at the expense of community are free to roam at will.

If the God of life is sovereign over every part of God's own creation, then to worship God is to love all of life as God loves it. Such love has no enemies, for all such designations are excluded from love. Enemies can exist only in dualistic or polytheistic faith systems, where it is believed that people are ruled by other, equally powerful tribal gods who have evil intentions. Ethical monotheism demands that all people be brought under the rule of the one God. Monotheism does not provide for enemies who are nonhuman and are categorized pejoratively as Krauts, Japs, V.C.'s, Commies. Those we classify as enemies are in fact our brothers and sisters, our mothers and fathers, our sons and daughters—members of our own family.

If God is one, then every war in human history is a civil war, for it has set the human family against itself. If that is so, nationalism must die. One's own nation cannot be regarded by the worshipers of

Yahweh as more sacred, more holy, and more righteous than any other. Any propaganda that would try to convince us otherwise must be countered in the name of the oneness of God.

It is tempting to the human psyche to desire, and even to promote, feuds or war, for enemies are useful. Enemies keep judgment turned outward. Enemies define and symbolize evil; hence they enable one to feel the passions of a crusade in the effort to eradicate such evil in the name of righteousness. As long as there is an enemy there will always be a recipient for those projected self-critical feelings that characterize human nature. When the human family divides in combat, both sides claim that theirs is the cause of righteousness. The universal God quickly becomes a tribal deity. The relatively recent criticism of war as an instrument of all participating nations' foreign policy carries with it a dawning ray of universalism. The persecution of peace proponents by their more "patriotic" critics indicates that universalism gnaws at the ancient tribal mentality of a premodern world.

Abraham Lincoln was once asked if he thought God was on the side of the North in the Civil War. He responded, "The real question is not whether God is on our side but whether we are on God's side." That is an answer that those who fly the flag of nationalism above their altars find disturbing. When we worship one God, we discover that we are called into a deeper understanding of the common humanity that binds us all. Nationalism is a lesser god, unable to bring its adherents into community with anyone outside the narrow boundary of a particular vision. No nation can live inside the Judeo-Christian faith tradition without seeing itself as standing under divine judgment. Worshipers of Yahweh will always know that their nation is not definitive.

Once we have glimpsed the oneness of God, we are forced to sacrifice many of the assumptions that have been made for God throughout history. The only holy God is not an adjunct to, nor a guarantor of, any particular way of life. God is not a bulwark for democracy. God does not exist to stand against communism. Human beings find their lives and values affirmed in particular political and economic systems. Then they invest those systems with claims of divinity or see them as expressions of the divine will, removing them thereby from judgment. That is idolatry, for no political system or economic structure is permanent. God is one. There is no other. This

God cannot be captured by our structures or used to support our lifestyles.

Another popular graven image surfaces when we analyze our religious life. Religious idolatry is subtle and insidious. It frequently wears the mask of piety and speaks with the accents of faith. Graven images are not just golden calves or carved Buddhas. Every visual representation of God promotes the bewitching temptation that presumes that the totality of God can be understood and controlled. This is a claim that many religious groups make. Well-meaning, devout people frequently presume to know more about God than we would ever claim for our own poetry or our scientific calculations. In both poetry and science we have learned that once we represent ideas by words, and concepts by pictures, limitations become obvious. With most of what motivates human behavior lying beneath the conscious mind, it is fair to say that we do not even understand ourselves or anyone else. Nor does anyone else understand us. Yet we are not bashful in making incredible claims about the wonder of God. Lonely, chaotic human lives are tempted to wrench God into definitions and symbols that we can deal with and to pretend that God will act according to our demands, and in recognizable ways. Religious people constantly delude themselves into believing that God is who they say God is, that God does what they say God does. The data of life are arranged to prove our suppositions. But in spite of our human protestations there can be no infallible revelations of the word or truth of God. No creed can define God. No church can contain all truth. The arcane mind of God confounds our finitude. When we fail to acknowledge that, we fall into idolatry.

The experience of worshiping one God opens life to the inner unity of the world and thereby enables us to accept life's diversity. Conversely, idolatry closes us and makes us defensive and imperialistic. Idols demands conformity of worshipers by suggesting that any deviation from the system is a deviation from God. Yet every theological system in Christian history is, at best, only a limited approximation of divine truth. The church as the guardian of the tradition tells the sacred stories and explains them, but the living out of those stories in the newness of time is a contemporary myth-revising process. There is truth in the Christian church, but the conceptualizations of that truth are forever both arguable and dated. The good news of the loving God in Christ continues to break into and through the arche-types of faith to live in the present moment. Christianity points to God. So do other religious traditions. But because every religious tradition is framed by human experience and shaped by human words, it never captures the God who is always beyond our human con-structions. The religious claims, made time and again throughout history by both large institutions and small splinter denominations, that the infallible or perfect truth of God is their solitary possession can be dismissed as audacious posturing in the quest for ecclesiastical power. Such claims are finally only expressions of idolatry. Modern religious graven images can include even creeds, scriptures, ex cathedra pronouncements, and sacred traditions.

"You shall have no other gods but me" is a call to live in responsible freedom. It is a call to live in this world without certainty, without any illusions, in the midst of life's inadequate and unknown dimensions. It is a call to live in the world without the assurance that any word, any phrase, any institution, or any system is totally trustworthy. It is a call to live without the rival siren songs of idols, to know that every revelation is shadowy.

Human frailty endlessly exacerbates the insecurity that manifests itself in our constant awareness of and fear of death. In an in-stantaneous thought or memory, feelings of inadequacy and self-doubt can destroy confidence. The impulse to cover or deny the abyss that threatens to engulf is understandably pervasive. Idols are ready and willing to rush into this breach, but they cannot, for idols are also subject to decay and insignificance. But the paradox of life is that the dark night of paralyzing fear is also the venue of the one God. "Though God slay me, yet will I trust," said Job through chattering teeth. The path into life goes *through* fear, not around it. Attempts to walk around the fear lead only to bondage—death through atrophy. Once having conquered fear of the God who has the power to deliver death as well as life, we no longer need to prove our worth. Yet we live in the denial of the birthright of our infinite worth that we are given by the God who wills us into life. When we are not at one with the infinite ground of being that we call God, then we are not at one with ourselves either. When we are not at one with ourselves, we will not be at one with anyone else.

The Bible calls this human condition sin. The Bible does not define sin as a deed; sin is a name for human life separated from the love of God and experiencing loneliness, inadequacy, and insecurity. The sinful response is our attempt to assemble the missing ingredients ourselves, and always at someone else's expense. Alienation is all around and through us and is seeping into future generations. Unable to love or be loved, our children repeat the patterns of compensation for despair, and so it goes to the third and fourth generation.

"You shall have no other gods before me." I am jealous. No one can take my place without corrupting my creation. The sins of the parents do get visited upon the children, the grandchildren, and the great-grandchildren, for sin is the constricting of life that comes when God is not flowing through us. Yahweh's demand is unconditional, exclusive, uncompromising, total. It is a divine picture of the meaning of creation that shows us the way life can and must be.

Sorry, my college bull-session friends! You are not innocent. Graven images you have created. So have we all.

Chapter 6

GOD'S HOLY NAME

"When I tell somebody my name, I have given him a hold over me that he did not have before. If he calls it out, I stop, look, and listen, whether I want to or not. In the book of Exodus God tells Moses that his name is Yahweh, and God has not had a peaceful moment since."
                                        —FREDERICK BUECHNER

The great American preacher Harry Emerson Fosdick was once invited to speak to a very hostile and tough group of striking coal miners in West Virginia. Fosdick had been warned that the miners had a habit of baiting preachers and that if he did not get the attention of his audience quickly, he could expect an uncomfortable evening. When Dr. Fosdick stood up in the public square to address his surly audience on a hot July night, he began his sermon in a rather startling fashion. "It's goddamn hot today," he said.

Suddenly that tough crowd of coal miners fell silent, their mouths open, as they wondered if they had really heard what they thought they had heard. Having won their attention. Fosdick continued, "That's what I heard a man say this morning," and from that provocative beginning, Dr. Fosdick launched into a passionate denunciation of profanity as a violation of the third commandment.

Most people, if asked to explain the meaning of "taking God's name in vain," would say it refers to profanity, especially profanity that uses the word "God." Yet the fact is that this note came into the commandment very late in its history and comprises only a small part of its historical and present meaning. The primary thrust of the commandment is not against profanity but against not keeping one's word. It focuses on the mystical meaning of a name.

We communicate both positive and negative feelings through our use of names. Many read the telephone directory as soon as it arrives to see if their names are spelled correctly. We feel a strange kind of devaluation when our names are publicly mispronounced. The ability to identify another by name is a major asset in almost every area of life.

In the late '60s a young lawyer named William Belser Spong, Jr., announced his intention to seek the Democratic nomination for the United States Senate from Virginia. Political wags suggested that with his name he was assured of the Chinese vote, hardly sufficient to ensure election. Despite his name he persevered, won the Democratic primary by a scant 611 votes, and defeated his Republican opponent in the general election to enter the Senate in 1967. Along with all the other freshman senators, this politican was invited to introduce himself to the media through the vehicle of a National Press Club luncheon. Each new senator was allowed two minutes to impress his name upon those who might well hold the key to any future political destiny. How does a politician indelibly project his name in two minutes? Senator Spong told of his personal concern for songwriters whose copyrights were regularly violated in Hong Kong. His first moral crusade as a senator, he announced, would be to sponsor legislation to halt such violations. Being a consensus politician, he had enlisted the support of the senior senator of Louisiana, whose name was Russell Long, and of the junior senator from Hawaii, whose name was Hiram Fong. Together they would author the Long, Fong, Spong, Hong Kong Song bill! After that, no commentator referred to him as Senator Sponge, which is what those who bear that name frequently get called.

Sometimes names are used to communicate images. Professional athletes know the value of an image. "Rocky" projects strength and power and is often a boxer's title. "Mean Joe Green" was a fearsome defensive lineman for the Pittsburgh Steelers. "The doctor" is the moniker preferred by Julius Erving of the Philadelphia 76ers and by the young New York Mets pitcher, Dwight Gooden, both of whom ply their trade like skilled surgeons. Joe Louis was known in the '30s as the "Brown Bomber," one of the first occasions in which skin color was marketed as a source of pride, a precursor of "black is beautiful."

We use nicknames to compliment and to insult. Slim, Shorty, and Fatty are among the human favorites. I once had a friend named Inky. He spent his first ten days of life in an incubator; that experience determined his name for a lifetime. Names have power—incredible power. "A rose by any other name would smell as sweet," wrote Shakespeare. Perhaps it would, but a name becomes a part of the identity of a human being. That name cannot be changed at whim without disturbing the substance of the individual.

The Hebrew people, more deeply than any other, understood the connection between identity and a name. They were intrigued by the mystique of a name. They reflected at length on the meaning and power of names. The word "name" appears in the Hebrew scriptures 750 times. "The name of Yahweh" is one of the most-used phrases in the biblical vocabulary. In the Book of Psalms alone, "the name of the Lord" occurs ninety-eight times. To the Hebrew mind, the name of the Lord was holy. Beyond that, the Hebrews viewed every name as significant, almost as an omen. A name was not merely a title; it conveyed the very nature of the thing named.

Throughout its pages the Bible carefully preserves a proper order about names, for to name someone or something was to assert that one had actual or potential power over that person or thing. The hierarchical order of domination is disclosed in the story of creation as God named Adam, who then named the animals. Adam also named the woman, for it was a patriarchal culture in which that story was written. Parents named their children. Men and women named mountains, plains, rivers, and cities. However, in the biblical story no one could name God. God told Moses his holy name, "I am," but from that moment of self-disclosure no one was allowed to speak that holy name. It was written as an unpronounceable set of letters: YHWH. When Hebrews came upon that holy symbol in the scriptures, they did not read "Yahweh," as we might do; rather, they recited the word "Adonai," which literally means "the Lord." Hebrews were taught that to speak the holy name was to defile Yahweh. No creature could possess God or have power over God, so no creature could utter the holy name.

Since, in the biblical story, a name was a clue to character, it was essential to change one's name if one's character changed. When Abram and Sarai were called to leave their home in Ur of the Chaldees to wander to a strange land where they were to give birth to a new nation, their names were changed: Abram to Abraham, Sarai to Sarah. Jacob wrestled at night with the angel by the brook Jabbok, and when he had proved his mettle and was ready to meet his destiny as the father of a new people, his name was changed from Jacob to Israel. The name Jacob meant "the one who supplanted." The name Israel meant "the one who would persevere and overcome." Israel gave his name to the nation that prevailed with God. When Saul of Tarsus saw the light on the road to Damascus and turned his life in a new direction, he became Paul the apostle. Simon bar Jonah confessed the name of the Christ who, upon seeing Simon's strength, renamed him Peter, the rock.

It was not uncommon for the prophets of Israel to speak their prophetic word through the naming of their children. Such children became the word of God enfleshed. One of those prophets was the first Isaiah, who lived at a time when the enemies of Judah were about to crush his nation. The tiny kingdom of Judah despaired of surviving the Assyrian onslaught. At that critical moment, Isaiah, the most respected prophet in Jerusalem, named his firstborn son Shear-jashub, "a remnant shall return": God will not allow the people of the covenant to be annihilated. A prophetic word was thus spoken through a name, through Isaiah's own surviving issue.

To address another by name was to claim either superiority or equality. To disclose one's name to another was to reveal one's character to that person. These nuances of meaning and attitude are present in the way in which the Bible deals with the elusive divine name of the God who is enigma, the God who is depth beyond penetration, height beyond perception, the God who is finally un-knowable except at those times and places when the veil parts in revelation to expose as much sacred mystery as the people can absorb. The Hebrews knew the boundaries of intellect and the limitations of subjective experience. They understood that the being of God was beyond every image, every claim, and every apprehension of God's nature. The name of God could not be spoken.

One of the hymns of the church catches this Hebrew insight with these words:

> Immortal, invisible God only wise,
> In light inaccessible hid from our eyes,
> Most blessed, most glorious, the Ancient of Days,
> Almighty, victorious, thy great name we praise.

Considering the theological importance given to names, in particular the name of God, it is reasonable to expect that one of the Commandments would constellate around the Hebrews' attitude towards God's name. The reverence for and primacy of the divine name is reflected in the prayer Jesus himself gave us to pray. The prayer begins with a name, "Father," that discloses the nature of divine relationship and is followed by a petition, "May your name be holy."

In the third commandment it is the holy name of God that ensures the corporate life of the covenant people. The prohibition against using this name in vain had little to do with profanity. It was, rather, an injunction calling the covenant people to integrity in their dealings with one another. The entire system of justice depended upon the sanctity of the word of those bound by that system.

The manner of arranging a legal contract in ancient Israel included first a period of negotiation or bargaining; haggling might be a better word. When an agreement was reached, the two parties would embrace and swear by the name of the Lord that they would be true to their word, that they would abide by their contract. Whoever broke the oath or violated the contract had taken the name of the Lord in vain; that is, he or she had rendered the divine name ineffective and valueless. In short, this commandment means: Keep your word. Live up to your agreements. Do not promise in God's name what you cannot accomplish.

The Hebrews recognized that human honor and the ability to trust the integrity and the word of another were necessary for an ordered society. Without adherence to this basic rule of community, life itself was no longer trustworthy and was reduced to a state of anarchy. Falsehood, deceit, and outright lies, either in public or private, shatter relationships. Truth is essential to the hope of a nation. When the leaders of a nation fail to embody this precept, they demonstrate the moral bankruptcy of that nation. Ability alone is not enough. A nation or a society in which people do not keep their word disintegrates.

The basic issue in this commandment is the power and sanctity of one's word spoken in the name of the Lord. God had chosen this nation to be God's witnesses, to become a beacon of light for all people. They were to be holy, a royal priesthood, a people signed with the mark of Yahweh (Exodus 19:5–6). In every human contact the people of the covenant were to be the bearers of the name of their God, and therefore bearers of God's quintessential life. Every act, every word, every thought of this nation was to be a reflection of the God to whom they belonged. The meaning of the third commandment was thus filtered into every aspect of life. It permeated all their words and actions, and even their honor. From the particularity of a legal oath taken in the name of the Lord the dictum spread to cover every transaction of every person who was a member of the covenant people.

Christians appropriated the concept for Christianity by supposing themselves the people of the new covenant. A Christian enters the new covenant through the act of baptism. It is by design and not coincidence that at baptism the neophyte receives a name by which he or she is known and then is baptized in another name, the name of God, now called by Christians not Yahweh but Trinity: Father, Son, and Holy Spirit. The symbol of that eternal name, the sign of the cross, is placed upon the foreheads of the newly baptized. This is the church's way of saying, "The name of Christ is now a part of the Christian's identification. From baptism on, everything one does, everything one says, everything one thinks, is a reflection upon the name that is worn." The sentimental attitude that restricts religion to increasingly smaller and more irrelevant segments of life is challenged by the overriding vision contained in this commandment.

"You shall not take the name of the Lord your God in vain" continued to be expanded in the Christian tradition. Jesus insisted that the word of the Christian ought to be simply yes or no, nothing more. Nothing additional is required of covenant people: no oath, no swearing by God or by holiness or by heaven above or by the earth beneath. The word of a disciple must always express the honesty that derives from the name of Christ that disciple confesses. The promises of baptism are binding till death.

The third commandment extends the second commandment's prohibition against idol worship. Just as the chosen people were not to use idols in attempts to control or manipulate God, neither were they to use the power of the divine name for magic or divination. To do so would be to assume the prerogative of God. This commandment also reminds us that it is human beings who respond to God's initiative, not the reverse. It warns human life against Promethean vanity, the impulse to steal the power and tools of the gods. While the first definition of "vain"—without value, force, or effect—is directed to the misuse of the name of God to give false oaths, to make promises that are broken or forgotten, the second definition of "vain" is "conceited, having an excessive regard for one's self." This second definition is better expressed in the Jerusalem Bible, which translates the commandment: "You shall not utter the name of Yahweh your God to misuse it, for Yahweh will not leave unpunished the person who utters his name to misuse it."

Early hearers of this commandment also understood misuse of the divine name to include misuse of the magical properties of the name. The commandment forbids invoking the divine name to either bless or curse, for such entreaties summon powers, both benevolent and malevolent, that are meant to affect the lives of the targets of those invocations.

This prohibition against blessing is followed in the Book of Common Prayer, where there are distinctions of language between the priestly blessings that are delivered by God's representative with the words "The blessing of God be upon *you*," and the blessing that can be offered in the liturgy by a member of the congregation with the words "The blessing of God be upon *us*." The agent of blessing is always God. No incantation or literary formula can release blessing. Only the God who blesses in historical experience, which is then called providence, possesses the power to bless. To bless is to confer life, and the source of all life is God.

The need for this restraint stems from the evolution of pagan religious practices in the second millennium B.C.E. Ancient peoples believed that the community was safeguarded by the blessings of the deity. Primitive religious belief also held that the deity's power was increased by the people's blessings. The community, therefore, used every opportunity to throw a protective net of blessing around itself and around the god it worshiped.

This third commandment cuts through that primitive belief that the tribal god needed certain cultic rites of blessing in order to preserve the god's divinity. The God of Israel did not depend on the community for divine power. The God of Israel was not "kept powerful" by correct liturgies that invested the divine nature with certain properties and characteristics. This commandment shifted worship from an obsessive concentration on finding the "right" formulas for blessing to a confidence in the God of all for protection.

Just as primitive superstitious religions supposed that human blessings safeguarded and strengthened both the community and its resident god, so also they believed that curses controlled evil destructive forces. The third commandment turned Israel away from superstition and toward reliance on the God who was sovereign over evil as well as good. Israelites were forbidden to use the name of Yahweh as a malediction on their enemies. Vengeance was the province of the Lord. It must have been difficult for those wandering nomads who were so vulnerable to war, disease, and the internal frictions that turn trivial incidents into insulting affronts, to change their ways. A time-honored method for protecting oneself against the curses and threats of others was to set curses against them, very much the way firefighters light a backfire to help control fire in open country. Fight fire with fire; cast a curse to repel a curse. It was a matter of self-defense.

In this commandment God forbids individuals to use such verbal weapons. The curses that appear in the Hebrew scriptures are said in the name of community, the covenant community through whom God speaks. Only God can curse, take revenge, vindicate oppressed people. The Psalms are full of laments that call upon God to come forth to bless and curse. That was God's part in the bargain. Job's friends taunted him to curse the name of the God who had failed to reward the just man. Job steadfastly refused, for to vilify the name of God was a heinous crime. To do so would have removed him from the covenant community and would have been an act of suicide. Jesus both broadened the meaning of truthfulness for the Christian community and added an expectation to the keeping of the commandment: "Bless those who curse you" (Luke 6:28). The way to be protected from evil is to return blessing for curse, good for evil.

With the empowering of the individual members of the Christian community through the Holy Spirit, the priesthood of all believers was now in evidence. Every baptized member could now be the vehicle of blessing and was expected to increase the storehouse of good in the world. It was no longer sufficient to merely ward off evil; Christians were to be vehicles of blessings. Even death, the last enemy, was to receive a response of blessing. Jesus responded to the curse of the cross with this blessing: "Father, forgive them for they know not what they do."

The distinction between blessings and curses that misuse the divine name, and blessings and curses that are spoken in response to the divine name, is finely drawn in the Christian scriptures. To discern the difference, one must turn inward and examine motivation. Is this blessing or curse done for love, or for mere survival? Is it done for the sake of the other, or for self? Is it consistent with the experience of the community of faith, or is it an anomaly that has no connection to the giver of life? Blessings and curses shape and mold the character of the one who speaks them, regardless of the effect on enemy or friend. The test of our own words is found in the health of our own souls.

What are we really saying when we say "goddamn" or "Go to hell"? Both indicate, if we literalize them, that we have usurped the place of God and that we are in a position to decide another's eternal destiny, that we have assessed exactly what another's life is worth. To appropriate the place of God by assigning a final destiny to another is to overstep the bounds of human possibility.

If we use the expression "for Christ's sake," we are claiming to be on the side of the angels. "For Christ's sake," we impatiently say, but we really mean "Get with it and be like me." The interchange of the human will for the divine will is self-idolatry.

The use of the divine name to assume divine power and control is blasphemy. Yet forgetting the primary meaning and retaining the curse language as expletive for any strong emotion has involved this commandment in a secondary way with profanity. Many a child has a vivid recollection of the taste of soap administered to wash out the "bad words" overheard by a parent or a guardian who reacted more from a concern for correctness in manners than from fear of "becoming as the gods." Many of us grew up knowing from an early age the distinctions between proper and improper vocabularly. Those "naughty" words also developed an alluring quality. Adolescent rebellion, the natural repudiation of parental protection and judgments, demands the breaking of rules in one way or another. Saying the forbidden words is one of the more innocuous forms of teenage mutiny. Some people never see it for what it is—the insurgency of maturation—and establish a lifelong habit. Others return to a lifestyle in which parental disapproval of swearing is interjected and becomes a part of the inherited value system.

Attempts to speak politely have corrupted and diluted the original language of profanity. The mild oaths "gosh," "my goodness," "merciful father" are all forms of "my God." The word "gee" is nothing except shorthand for Jesus. Even the phrase "for crying out loud" originally was a reference to Jesus on the cross. The most fastidious among us invent expletives that do not call for definition, such as "sugar" and "Jiminy Cricket." Beyond refined manners, however, there is an objective response. The words "God," "Jesus," and "Christ" represent the most sacred realities the Christian knows. The profane use of these holy words is an insensitive offense to that centering faith.

Profanity trips off the lips of some people with such ease and with so little meaning that it is clearly of little significance to them. For others, it is the only legitimate vocabulary of anger, and nothing else quite serves the purpose. For still others, it is blasphemous, an almost unforgivable sin. It is interesting that most of our oaths and obscenities have either a religious or a sexual content. It is both curious and significant that the most intimate human experiences, our vowed relationships with our God and with the ones we love, provide the vocabulary of profanity.

Profanity expresses a kind of bankruptcy of language, for our profane symbols lose their meaning in very loose context. People have been excoriated for being as "stupid as hell" and as "smart as hell." We cannot be both. Objects are described as "big as hell" and "little as hell." The weather is called "hot as hell" and "cold as hell." All are mutually exclusive images. Language that casual and imprecise is frankly meaningless.

When symbols are literalized, there is sometimes a startling effect. A story is told about a man in a bar who looked up and saw a fellow drinker who appeared to be familiar. "Where in hell have I seen you before?" he inquired. To which the stranger responded, "I don't know. What part of hell do you come from?"

Undoubtedly, profanity has some therapeutic value. We discharge emotion, hostility, and anger with our expletives, and it is better to express these feelings verbally than to attack another physically.

I once regularly played squash with an orthopedic surgeon, a man of furious temper and massive frame. He was also well known for an uncompromised willingness to use purple prose to give full verbal expression to his feelings. His manner revealed little gentility or grace either on or off the court. When playing squash, he wanted only to hit that ball as hard as he could, and when he missed a shot, he would hurl a verbal oath out that could be heard a city block away. All his oaths began with "goddamn!" About midway through a match one day, I stopped the game and said, "How about swearing at your profession instead of mine, for a while? Next time you miss a shot, instead of taking it out on God, scream, 'I hate aspirin.'" He agreed to try. A minute later, when his ball hit the tin, he shouted, "Goddamn it, I hate aspirin!" I thought that it was a partial victory.

Profanity is not a critical area of human behavior; it does not fall into the categories of crime or vice. But habitual use of it does reflect a character that is rebellious, casual, or even perhaps violent. The real substance of this commandment, however, lies elsewhere. It refers to the validity of one's word. That is important, for the very matrix of society is the assumption that a person's word is good and that one can expect honesty in human interchange.

Chapter 7

THE MARKING OF TIME

"Every day is a god, each day is a god, and holiness holds forth in time."
—ANNIE DILLARD

In the strict homes of the Calvinistic South, Sunday was called the Sabbath. That name, lifted from Jewish tradition, was applied to the day of the week set apart by Christians for worship. In such homes Sunday/Sabbath was a most unpleasant day, especially for active little children. It was a day on which religious customs prevented children from being normal. Sunday was such a day for me. Sunday/Sabbath meant special clothes—not school clothes or play clothes, but Sunday clothes—fancy, stiff, restrictive clothes that one dared not dirty or tear. And the inevitable trip to Sunday school came next, a trip that did not seem to be required of adults.

Sunday school was a chore for me. I confess that I entered the ministry in spite of my Sunday-school training and not because of it. When I am pressed to recall anything from my Sunday school experiences, only personal memories of a particular teacher or of a gimmick such as a perfect attendance pin come to me. Little content remains.

After Sunday school, the day wore on with unrelieved, oppressive expectations. I was not allowed to remove Sunday clothes—very effective behavior control. Almost anything that was fun was prohibited: no marbles, no tag or baseball, not even roll-a-bat. Movies were out. Things like movies made it necessary for others to work, I was told. Games, especially card games, were the work of the devil. Television was not yet invented. To my childish eyes, the adults seemed to be doing the things they wanted to do; only the kids were placed on Sabbath day restrictions. Perhaps only kids have to keep the Sabbath, I thought. Maybe the Sabbath will be like an allergy that can be outgrown in time.

Sundays dragged on interminably, boring me beyond endurance. Positive activities included visiting relatives I really did not want to see, and reading. There was strong encouragement to read the Bible, but those thin little golden-edged pages constantly stuck together or creased or tore. They seemed never to turn for my little fingers. And the language of that book, with the "thees," "thous," "asketh," and "beggeths" was, to my young mind, incomprehensible at best and silly at worst. Some of my negativity toward the King James Bible was born on those Sunday afternoons.

How could a child reared in this atmosphere learn to love God? God was portrayed as a stern heavenly father who spent his time telling children what they could not do or punishing them if they ever did it. God could never have been a child, was my conclusion, for God did not know what fun was, nor did God ever smile behind that long beard. I asked my mother once why Sundays were so different, so dull and boring. "Well, dear," mother responded, "Sunday is the Lord's day." In my mind anyone who had a day like that just could not be very nice, certainly not exciting or interesting.

Of course, I could not admit those feelings, for a healthy dose of the fear of God had been instilled in me. I grew up coerced into doing the religious thing and resenting every minute of it. Weekends were ruined because Sunday was a part of every weekend. Imagine my delight and surprise when I discovered that there was not one biblical injunction anywhere in any of the sixty-six books of holy scripture that placed prohibitions on Sunday—not one. Sabbath and Sunday are not the same. They never have been the same.

The sabbath was the Jewish day of rest and was identified late in Hebrew history as a weekly seventh-day observance. Sunday was never the seventh day, the day of rest. Sunday was the Christian day of resurrection. It was the day on which God acted, the first day of the week, not the last. Sunday as a Christian holy day was originally marked not by withdrawal and rest but by celebration, festivity, parties. Observance of the Lord's Supper, which very quickly became the designated service of worship for Christian people on their holy day, was festive. This is why that service was and is called a "celebration" of holy communion.

Early in Christian history the Jewish sabbath—the day of rest and the last day of the week—and the Christian Sunday—the day of celebration and the first day of the week—existed side by side. Early Jewish Christians observed both, and the two were never confused.

Sabbath emphasized the cessation of labor and normal activity; Sunday emphasized festivity. But as Christianity moved away from its Jewish roots and into the Gentile world, observance of the sabbath, with its cultic ceremonial and judicial precepts, faded. Sunday, the celebration of God's re-creating work in the resurrection event, dominated. There were many ebbs and flows in the Christian Sunday tradition over the centuries. The concept of rest was reintroduced into feudal society. Sunday was the one day the serfs did not labor for the lord of the manor, but it was a fluid tradition, without a set practice.

Then along came John Calvin. John Calvin must have been exactly like my childish images of God: stern, long-faced, somber, boring, rigid, humorless. Calvin was undoubtedly one of the great minds of Christian history, but he was not a scintillating theologian. This man served a God who ruled by rigid legalistic regulations and judgments. John Calvin, more than anyone else in Christian history, lifted the ancient Hebrew sabbath day tradition out of the past, with all its restrictions, its admonitions to rest, and its restraints on activity, and imposed it on the Christian Sunday. By merging the most inhibiting aspects of the seventh- and first-day traditions, Calvin transformed the character of the Christian Sunday in the most legalistic and constricting way. It was John Calvin's creation that I experienced on the first day of each week as a child. John Calvin's Sunday: rest from your labor; no fun today; church is a somber experience where laughter is sinful and worship is mournful; be quiet; this is God's house; stiff clothes; no marbles; no baseball. None of that was originally part of the day of the resurrection.

What joy it was to discover that this kind of Sunday was rooted in the work of John Calvin and was not found in the Christian scriptures or early Christian traditions! The Christian Sunday is not the ancient Hebrew sabbath with its stylized disciplines, though a change of pace, a break in routine, a setting aside of daily occupation is implicit in all marking of sacred time.

Even the sabbath tradition has roots that were considerably transformed over time. "Remember the Sabbath and keep it holy" became part of the consensual law at Sinai. The remainder of the sabbath tradition was editorial expansion. In the Deuteronomic version of the Ten Commandments, for example, the sabbath is identified not with the creation but with the Exodus. The Deuteronomic writer enjoins the sabbath day of rest upon Israel and upon every life that the people of Israel touch—citizens and slaves, human beings and beasts of burden—because, says Deuteronomy, rest is essential to life. No living creature, regardless of station or condition, should be abused. Do not forget, says the book of Deuteronomy, that you were slaves, oppressed in Egypt. Remember that periodic rest from labor is a right of every human being and every living thing. It is not a privilege that one generously bestows; it is a right guaranteed by God.

The priestly writer carried this idea a step further by introducing a creation story from the oral tradition in which God is the model for the seven-day and work-and-rest pattern. We not only obey God; we act as God acts. Before the commandment was interpreted and fashioned by the more sophisticated pre- and post-exilic editors, we can say only that the wilderness people observed a sabbath. It may have taken forms similar to those observed of the nature religions that predominated all around them. Typically, lunar festivals were monthly celebrations of the new moon. Such festivals provided times when ordinary routines and taboos were suspended. If these festivals were ever described as rest, the rest would have been characterized by change of pace, not by inactivity. Festivals were and are a time to indulge the passions, to cut loose.

There has been some speculation by scholars that Moses' time in Midian exposed him to ironsmiths who needed to bank their fires periodically. These may have been times of rest from work that allowed the forges to cool down and gave opportunity for honoring the fire gods. In a polytheistic society where lunar deities also were worshiped, the lunar cycle naturally fell into seven-day segments that gave a rhythm to the work of the smiths. But all this is conjecture; we really do not know how the seven-day sabbath tradition began.

That the ancient Hebrews observed sabbath is fairly certain. But *how* they observed holy time is reasoned speculation, deduced from the findings of various disciplines. The Hebrews incorporated their neighbors' religions by re-imaging and reinterpreting them within their own religious framework. Their ethical monotheism drew all things into the mind and breath of God. Even time was a creature of God; and so on the sabbath the Hebrew people deliberately and self-consciously, in the words of the old hymn, "took time to be holy." Sabbath gave their life a rhythm, a self-conscious quality of worship, a making worthy the whole of their existence. The progression of the tradition moved from what was perhaps an astrologically determined festival with characteristics of nature worship, to a weekly festival marked by an absence of work. Then the Hebrews adopted the seven-day creation story overlaid with rigid injunctions and specific definitions that prohibited work.

In the period of the exile these definitions and prohibitions met the identity and survival needs of the people. These Babylonian captives had been uprooted from their native soil, torn away from their sacred tradition, and separated from Jerusalem, the center of national and religious life. The deepest threat faced by these prisoners of war was the threat of assimilation, of losing themselves in the dominant and more urbane culture of Babylon.

It was the practice of the Babylonians to bring the leaders of a conquered land to Babylonia but to leave the poor and unskilled in their devastated homeland to survive as best they could. This policy would prevent uprisings, they reasoned, and also gave them the best of the vanquished nation's human treasure for their own use. But it also gave the captured community an opportunity to consolidate and reform in concentrated and unusual circumstances.

This is precisely what happened under the leadership of prophets such as Ezekiel and of the exiled temple priesthood. Two customs that were revived became the identifying signs of Judaism. It was from this time that the covenant people were spoken of as Jews rather than Hebrews. The Yehudi (of the tribe or kingdom of Judah) were the people of the exile. As their name changed, so did their practices. The reinstated rituals of circumcision and the rigidly enforced observance of a weekly sabbath separated them as non-Babylonians and unified them as Jews. The seven-day creation story was selected and written down to support the new emphasis on sabbath and to give it a divine imprimatur. In other words, the Jews probably observed the sabbath and then selected the seven-day creation story to give it a theological basis of origin, not the other way around.

The two customs, circumcision and sabbath observance, made the set-apartness of the Jews obvious. On the body of every Jewish male was the sign of his Judaism; and on each seventh day every Jew became publicly discernible when labor and commerce ceased in the captive community.

Circumcision and regular sabbath observance renewed life for the exiles. No religion is more than a generation away from extinction if its story is forgotten. No one could be a member of the covenant people, either by birth or by adoption, unless the tale of God's rescue and the people's response to their redemption was known and appropriated. Circumcision was a visible reminder of the Mosaic covenant and of the Exodus story that was, and is, the heart story of Judaism. Sabbath worship called the people together to remind them and to reacquaint them with their primary identity as a people of God. The liturgy centered on the word, the retelling of the saving events of God and God's people. It constantly reminded them that their true home was not in exotic and seductive Babylonia but in the land that the Lord God had promised would always be their own. This promised land was the place where they could truly be themselves—free and blessed. In exile they were removed from all the natural reminders of their history: the landscape with its fabled mountains and rivers, the towns, the plains populated with ghosts of past heroic deeds, and Jerusalem, the golden city, the place where the messiah was awaited. In exile new ways of living the story and imagining a future whose destiny was contained in those ancient accounts had to be imposed on the alien culture. "How can we sing the Lord's song in a foreign land?" they mourned. Well, they did sing it, although everyone came to know it was a makeshift tune. One day they would return.

In the process of national reformation that the exiles' extreme duress required, a zealous scrupulosity crept into religious life, particularly into the rules of sabbath observance. Under pressure from the Jewish leadership, sabbath laws were defined and redefined. Thirty-nine different kinds of work were specifically prohibited. No medical attention for chronic or non-emergency situations was allowed. Five centuries later dutiful priests, carrying on and refining the punctilious exile traditions throughout that rabbinic period, castigated Jesus for healing the man with the withered hand on the sabbath. A withered hand is a chronic, not an emergency, situation, they insisted, and thus judged Jesus guilty of breaking the sabbath. Broken bones could not be set on the sabbath, for even though it might be painful, a broken bone in the arm or leg would not normally cause death.

No embalming of the dead was allowed on the sabbath. The enactment of this law became part of the passion narrative when Jesus was taken from his cross on Friday so that his friends could avoid the defiling work of removing the body on the sabbath, which began at sundown on Friday. There was also no time to embalm, so the body was wrapped in a linen shroud and placed in the tomb. At dawn on the first day of the week, the women came to the tomb bearing spices for embalming. They came as soon as they could see to travel after sabbath had ended.

There was a rule against walking more than three-fifths of a mile beyond the borders of the town on the sabbath, this being the distance a priest had to walk to accomplish his sabbath-day duties. For a Jew to walk more than that distance broke the injunction to refrain from work. The book of Acts refers to the Mount of Olives as a sabbath day's journey from Jerusalem—that is, three-fifths of a mile. Even now Hasidic Jews restrict their sabbath travel to that distance. They have further restricted themselves by limiting their mode of travel to walking.

The importance of sabbath liturgical practice grew out of a deep human need to know oneself in relationship to the source of life. This commandment is grounded in the necessity to act out the most important life-giving, centering drama of our lives. Worship demands that the human spirit turn from routines and take time to be reminded of and related to that which creates, orders, and sustains life. To be re-created and renewed requires time and self-conscious practice.

The sabbath was institutionalized in Judaism to enable this quality of rest and communion with the divine to become explicit, real, habitual, and central to Jewish life. When the Jews finally settled on a seven-day week ending in the sabbath, thus establishing as intentional rhythm of life, they numbered the other days with reference to the sabbath. Monday was the second day after sabbath, Thursday was the fifth day after sabbath, and so on. The religious genius of those slaves who knew themselves as chosen was their insight into the divine-human relationship. Through their response to their God they came to understand much about the human condition. The fact is that all people need a sabbath, a day of withdrawal from life's routines, a day to contemplate the holy self-consciously.

That time of withdrawal was legislated in colonial America by the Christian majority with the passage of the so-called "blue laws." The sale of goods on Sunday was forbidden. As the country grew, blue laws were redefined to refer only to non-emergency goods. The local ordinances that categorized emergency and nonemergency items were as convoluted and intricate as any sabbath midrash. But these laws are being rescinded as society becomes more pluralistic and secular.

Increased affluence and leisure time have changed the rhythm of the week. Most employers do not expect their employees to work more than five days per week; the Saturday and Sunday weekend meets the intent of sabbath to provide a regular break from work. As many Americans do not work at physically demanding jobs, the work break is not rest in the usual sense of that word. Rest from work more often means a refreshing and recreational use of time. Sabbath rest has become weekend leisure.

But sabbath is more than rest. It is also worship. It is a time to engage in regular, habitual, disciplined behavior that is character-forming. Leisure-time activities, like sabbath worship, also shape and reflect the values of individuals and society. The typical activities of the secular sabbath, sports and shopping, indicate that competition and consumerism are prominent components of contemporary life. The secular temples in which we celebrate winning and owning are athletic stadiums and shopping malls.

Neither sabbath worship nor weekend leisure is a private activity. Just as self-consciously religious people gather in congregations to worship, so those who honor the secular sabbath associate and share leisure time with others. There is a human tendency expressed both inside and outside church life for like-minded people to come together. We spend our leisure with people we find comfortable and familiar. Our friends are few, not many. This is the norm for voluntary associations. In secular groupings exclusivity is assumed. In church groups, however, exclusivity is challenged by a gospel that is inclusive and universal.

Sabbath is the time to re-create ourselves as the people of God. An intentional sabbath provides solitude for reflection and time in welcoming communities where values are shared and stories are told about who we are and who we might become. Sabbath is the time when the best food and drink are served in love from a table where all are welcome. It is a time to see life as it really is—holy.

Chapter 8

CLAIMING OUR INHERITANCE

"We all come from the past, and children ought to know what it was that went into their making, to know that life is a braided cord of humanity stretching up from time long gone, and that it cannot be defined by the span of a single journey from diaper to shroud."

—RUSSELL BAKER

"Where have all the heroes gone?" The response to that question comes to us through surveys that have collected the names of contemporary heroes. Those reports make nervous reading, for such lists reflects dominant cultural values. Recent lists are heavy with the names of movie and rock stars. Those who have become rich and famous of their own efforts are always represented on our lists as examples of the "American dream" that promises success without regard to class or parentage. As we name our heroes in these latter years of the century, women and blacks are more prominent, military and sports figures less frequent, than in preceding generations. We continue to revere those people who have lived their lives with charity and vision—people such as Abraham Lincoln, Albert Einstein, Martin Luther King, and Mother Teresa—people who were and are respected by both their enemies and their supporters for their personal integrity and what might be called moral soul force.

Recently, students at the University of Wisconsin were asked to list their top five heroes, male and female. To the researchers' surprise, the students' mothers and fathers were the most frequent first choices. Often grandfathers were listed, as were religious figures. Interpreters of the data announced that this represented a turn toward conservatism in the young. Perhaps. Or it could mean a parental willingness to become heroes to their own children, to be their models of strength and courage rather than encourage them to search further for elusive prototypes of either virtue or ease.

The covenant people of Sinai would not have been surprised by the inclusion of parents in any listing of heroic figures. They expected parents to be heroes of the faith. The fifth commandment lifts that expectation by presenting parents as connecting links between the faith once delivered and the faith lived out with its social consequences for present and future generations.

The Ten Commandments fall into two divisions. The first grouping contains those precepts that refer to the nature of God and the recognition of the covenant relationship. The second grouping spells out those rules that regulate social interaction among the covenant people. The fifth commandment to honor parents is commonly misunderstood as the first of six communal rules. It more properly is a pivotal commandment that links the God of the covenant to the social life of the people. In this dual role, it participates both in the statement of belief—the theology—and in the consequences of that belief—the behavior of the individual as it contributes to the group life.

In both the theological and the social contexts, no individualistic motif was meant when this commandment was delivered to the whole of the community. Its intent was to keep the community intact as a people of God who would be unified in belief and formed through a code of behavior proceeding from that belief. The theological component of parental honor, from which the social explication is derived, speaks to the community's relationship to YHWH, as do the preceding four commandments. There might be a temptation at this point to relate mother/father to God and to digress into a feminist, wholistic, or Eastern argument about the totality of the divine nature and into a discussion of human personality and destiny as a manifestation of divine attributes. However, these are psychological interpersonal concerns of twentieth-century Western civilization that are highly individualistic and personal in thrust.

In recent years there again has been great optimism about the human personality's ability to develop and grow into its full creative potential. Liberal religion values independence, even autonomy; it holds the development of individual potential as its highest good. Becoming all that we are capable of becoming is God's will for our lives.

Conservative religion, on the other hand, calls for conforming life patterns, especially for work and relational designs that repeat the past and are stabilizing and familiar. However, conservative religion promotes a kind of piety where one's relationship with God is primarily individualistic, a relationship that supersedes all other demands and intimacies.

Individualism in either its conservative or its liberal form was unknown to the ancient Hebrews. They lived collectively and communally. Individuals who broke with tradition, who refused to respond to the expectations of the society in which they lived, were few. Such people either became outcasts, living on the fringes, often dying when cut off from the life-sustaining community, or else they were leaders who brought their entire community into their new way of thinking and acting. Abraham's decision not to kill his firstborn son was a radical denial of his inherited role (Genesis 22). As tribal leader, he was expected to sacrifice his son so that the entire community would receive the protection and favor of the tribal god. His life-affirming action re-visioned not only the role of leadership but the nature of God as well. The covenant God was a god of mercy, not sacrifice.

Those rare individuals who were willing to shake the foundations of society, who put God to the test as well as themselves, were remembered as people who had looked upon the face of God and lived. The undertaking was so dangerous that there was no encouragement for others to follow their lead.

The story of Uzzah (2 Samuel 6) tells of a person who accompanied the ark of the covenant back to Jerusalem at David's command and was struck dead for coming too close to holiness as he reached out to steady the tilting ark on the rocky road. God's holiness consumes mere mortals, say the sacred stories. Direct encounters with God were thus discouraged. Individual piety and individualism as a lifestyle were anathema and, except for a chosen few, led to death.

As these Commandments are intended for a tribal society rather than for an individualistic mentality, premature digressions into twentieth-century thought patterns would not be consistent with ancient Hebrew mind-sets.

The mother and father, in this commandment's original theological perspective, were the matriarchs and patriarchs of the faith. They were people who responded as the chosen of the holy one and who entered into the covenant relationship that drew the ragtag, scattered Habiru (wandering nomads) into a monotheist ethical society for which good was centered in community worship. Honor to one's biological parents was expected as long as those parents handed down the sacred tradition. Parents were honored primarily because they were the storytellers. They knew the places, the events, the encounters with El Elyon, El Shaddai, Adonai, Elohim—former names of the one who finally became the "I Am"—the one who never deserted them and who promised to make them into a holy people. That promise could not be completed in a single generation. It would require countless generations of "parents" who would keep the memory alive, who would remind their children of their chosenness. The stories themselves told of God's saving work in history. They also told of those protoparents, Abraham and Sarah, Isaac and Rebecca, Jacob and his wives, who set the story in motion and whose children carried it forward because it was their duty as parents and as the people of God.

This line of storytellers, our spiritual parents who transmit identity, is recounted in the Christian letter to the Hebrews. At the end of the litany the author writes, "These are all heroes of faith, but they did not receive what was promised, since God had made provision for us to have something better, and they were not to reach perfection except with us" (Hebrews 11:40, Jerusalem Bible). Centuries after Sinai, early Christians continued to honor their covenanting parents by recognizing that God's plan of salvation is for all people.

In order to follow this commandment to honor them we must first know who our parents are. All of us live within stories of our choosing. Who are our spiritual parents, our heroes? Are they presidents, saints, inventors, artists? All have stories upon which we might model our lives. The test of the story in terms of the fifth commandment is its conformity to covenant. Nationalism, family pride, creativity, and piety all fail as central themes. The themes of covenant are justice, mercy, peace, and hope enacted within a relationship with God and motivated and empowered by that relationship.

We live our lives within the context of many stories. Certainly our family stories, national stories, institutional stories (church, school, club, Scouts, for instance) are important. For Christians and Jews, however, the overarching covenant story is the one that centers and binds us. That story and the witness of those we honor in it give us the courage to revise our lesser stories. We need courage to say no to any parent, government, or church demands that are contrary to the command "to act justly, to love tenderly and to walk humbly with your

God" (Micah 6:8, JB). These activities of honor connect us to those Sinai people. As it was for them, so it is for us. The call of the covenant pierces time and space and draws us into common identification as the people of God related through our spiritual parents.

Having established the parental duty as one that preserves the covenant relationship, and the filial duty as giving honor to the keepers of the religious tradition, the commandment then pivots from those injunctions that focus on our duty toward God to focus on our duty toward neighbor, beginning with the intimate relationship between children and their parents. It is interesting that this is the only one of the social commandments that is cast in a positive construct. Commandments six through ten place restraints and controls upon our behavior. "You shall not kill." "You shall not commit adultery." "You shall not steal." This commandment to honor, however, calls us to positive behavior.

Since laws exist primarily to curb human behavior, the commandment assumes difficulty in familial relationship. It is not easy or even instinctual to love one's parents. Despite a cultural bias for a nostalgic, romantic idealization of both motherhood and fatherhood, loyalty and love are not automatic responses to blood ties.

The data that contradict the commonly held belief that family love is natural begin with a look at the animal world. Human beings as part of the animal world should not be surprised to observe behavior in themselves similar to that found in lower forms of life. One of the primary marks that distinguish the reptile world from the mammal world is that reptiles are generally nonnurturing and hostile to their own hatched offspring, frequently to the point of murder. Mammals gained some evolutionary advantage by beginning to tend and care for their young. However, most mammals do not extend care beyond the physiological tasks of conceiving, giving birth, early nurturing, and weaning. Once an animal is weaned, the young of few species continue any relationship with parents or even acknowledge that there was ever anything special about the parental relationship. In the animal world, full-grown offspring do not depend on the parents and there is no parent-child relationship once the offspring attain independence.

In the human species the child is able to survive alone physically after puberty. Throughout most of human history (and this is still a normal pattern in many cultures) the child becomes an adult in the early teen years. However, advanced and economically privileged societies prolong adolescence until the child is educated and able to achieve economic as well as physical independence from the parent. As long as a child relies on the parent for survival, no law is necessary. It is at the point of emancipation from the supporting and confining parental home that humans depart from the patterns of the rest of the animal kingdom. Even when there is no biological or economic necessity to interact, a majority of adult children continue to relate to their parents; so this is an acquired behavioral characteristic of civilization.

When we look at anthropological studies of primitive societies, we make a somewhat startling discovery: economic factors dictate ethical behavior norms, particularly those norms that relate to the intergenerational relationship. Economic factors dictated the elimination of the elderly in some ancient tribes. Those who were unable to share the physical burden of the struggle for survival were not carried by the tribe, even as elderly sages or genealogical storytellers. Anyone who was strong enough to survive to an old age (a rare occurrence in primitive societies) could be treated shamefully without its bothering anyone's conscience. In some cultures, such persons were ejected from the tribe, left to starve, or even placed at the mercy of hungry wolves.

In these survival societies there was little devotion to parents either. Courtesy, respect, and consideration for elders appear then to be learned characteristics, not instinctual. Certainly they are not universal or normative responses in human life, either present or past.

The insights of depth psychology have confirmed the major themes of ancient mythology. The rivalry and overt hostility that mark the parent-child relationship, particularly as the child reaches maturity, are documented in clinical case studies that reproduce the motifs of Oedipus, Electra, and Persephone—three whose parents made growing up difficult. The model of perfect parenting to which we aspire is part of the thin veneer of civilization that conceals intense human emotions. In both the psychological and the biological maturation process, it is the child's duty and destiny to replace the parent. The ensuing rivalry raises guilt in the children as they mature. As the younger generation assumes responsibility, the power of the parent is reduced. A parent being confronted by a son or daughter who is ready and willing to take the parent's place is shaken by intimations of mortality, or what Paul Tillich called the threat of nonbeing. It is the aging parent's fate to lose power and status and to sacrifice position, a loss that triggers fear and hostility in the parent. These turbulent emotions, while a part of life, usually remain unspoken. Families commonly live out the conflicts and complexes of their internal jealous competitions in hidden ways.

When we consider the strong feelings that swirl around the primary relationships, psychology and theology collide. Sigmund Freud, through his seminal work in the passions of the mind, caused us to consider the probability that in some manner every son lives out the myth of Oedipus, the king who fell in love with his mother after killing his father. Freud identified patricide, the wish if not the act, with original sin. He went so far as to explain the Eucharist as a totem ritual in which the murderous child incorporated the flesh and blood of the powerful parent (God in Christ) in order to take on the characteristics of the murder victim.

Neither psychologists nor theologians have presented an adequate myth for the daughter/parent conflict. Since independence has not been considered a virtue in females, who have historically moved their dependencies from fathers to husbands (or to the male-dominated "mother" church in the case of women religious), parental conflicts tend to be played out in more subtle and less easily observed ways.

The feminist movement in this century has cast about for adequate myths that portray the woman whose development is not arrested and who strives for independence from parental authority. Again, such a myth would spin a narrative of original sin if becoming an adult means assuming the power and responsibilities of the parent who is ambivalent about relinquishing such power and responsibility. Adulthood is not only given; it is taken.

The Judeo-Christian tradition provides such a myth in the creation story of Genesis 2. In that story, home (the garden) is comfortable. The father God has provided for all needs. God has also provided the means of expulsion/escape. The fruit of the tree, identified as the knowledge of good and evil, when eaten will confer wisdom. Knowing means entering into awareness, including awareness of death. It also means coming to a consciousness that expands human existence through imagination and the development of skills that are motivated by the urgency that finite life places upon us. Eve, the central actor in this myth, usurps parental power and responsibility. She and Adam, who must now provide for themselves, are cast out and enter into the world as it really is and has been all along. In both the Oedipus and Eve stories the bid for separation from the (male) parent is identified as original sin. The moral ambivalence continues in Eve's story; early church fathers cursed her for bringing death into the world and causing the death of God in Jesus. But they also blessed her, for there would have been no mighty act of redemption had there been no fall from grace.

Separation from the mother has not taken on the mythic proportions of the child-father conflict. That may be because the wife-mother has followed her male protector's orbit, and so a break from the paternal relationship means a separation from both parents. If women are to have a story that leads them into independence, then there must be a model of a mother who is powerful and responsible. Mary is the only one to whom Christian women might turn, but she has been presented in Christian piety as an unassuming, obedient girl. Women have been encouraged to imitate her fabled virginity and innocence. In order to become women of power and authority, Christian women must either rebel against the child-bride image or else refashion the Mary myth as a story about a woman who was able to fly in the face of convention and live out the destiny of adult status that was uniquely hers. Her destiny did not rest solely on a dependent relationship with husband, father, or mother.

It is only when children become adults and so peers of their parents that the adult parent/child relationship can easily be one of honor. The commandment speaks to those whose separation is incomplete and who harbor resentment, envy, fear, even hatred, as well as affection, gratitude, and love. Until full maturity is achieved, the negative emotions motivate behavior. For that reason the commandment demands honor, a behavior that can be willed, not love, an emotion that cannot be willed. The commandment calls for honor in spite of the corresponding ambivalent emotions that emanate from a parent who may resent as well as admire the child's prowess.

People who come to counselors and pastors often tell how much they love their parents. Yet while protesting their devotion they grip the arms of the chair until the whites of their knuckles show. Pastors learn to read body language as carefully as they listen to words.

Counselors are aware of the hostile jealousy between mother and daughter that is particularly intensified when the mother begins to reach the menopause years just as the daughter blooms into the fullness of her feminine form. A similar hostility marks the father-son relationship as a father's physical strength wanes and his son overtakes him. The first time a son defeats his father in some competitive enterprise is celebrated by the son, remembered by the father. Indeed, to look through the romantic, wishful sentimentality that surrounds the culture's observance of motherhood and fatherhood is to find something quite different from sustained love and devotion. Examine the references to mother in profanity, for example. A "son of a what" do we call one another? A "mother what"? Our profanity reveals our underlying, ambivalent, hidden feelings.

In the lyrics of country and western ballads, mother is sung about with the same kind of deep, touching emotions that are directed to God and faithful dogs—"Old Shep." It escapes the casual listener that most country and western songs are about the death of mother. There is no doubt that the relationship between the grown child and the parent is one of love and hate, of dependency and rebellion, of closeness and distance, of guilt and affection.

Sentimentality, as opposed to sincerity, is a cover for unacceptable hostility that we are not willing to face. No celebration is more sentimental than our culture's observance of Mother's Day and Father's Day. The great devotion to parents that is couched in poetry and song is partially an effort to cover a deep and abiding antipathy between the generations. An examination of the motives present when a son or daughter "gives up his or her life to care for mother" uncovers something more than love. Emotional dependency breeds hostility on both sides. Possessive parents produce dependent children who dutifully care for their parents but all the while harbor great amounts of anger that is usually buried in the unconscious. Few people can finally love the person upon whom they are dependent, and some word or deed will slip out to betray them. Many "accidents" that befall elderly people are not so accidental as they might seem. Less socially acceptable hostilities are evident in the increase of reported physical assaults and batterings of aged parents. The Hebrew people seemed to understand this, and so in their most sacred ten words they have challenged us in the name of God to set aside the inner conflicts and honor those who have passed on to us the gift of life. The fifth commandment assumes that the honoring of parents is a calling to a higher way than innate behavior would produce. It is honor, not mawkish pretense, that keeps parents safe from rejection and the hostility that accompanies rivalry.

Some people will spurn the notion of hostility toward parents as nonsense. Some will be angered at the very idea, because awareness of the dark side of life is unpleasant. Some will feel compelled to assert that their parents were perfect parents for whom there was unabated affection, but that is because it is so painful to face the reality of our own inner hostility. It is all the more difficult after death removes the possibility of resolution; the need to keep memory unsullied distorts the past or disturbs the peaceful present. Yet when these ideas are verbalized in public forums, an uneasy restlessness almost always ripples through the audience. These waves of recognition are feelings most of us would prefer to ignore, feelings that are not only real but buried in the very heart of life. In their non-neurotic forms, these ambivalent emotions erupt in adolescent rebellion. Teenagers suddenly decide that their parents do not know anything about anything and are probably the most ignorant adults in the world; when these teenagers reach young adulthood they are quite surprised by how much their parents were able to learn in so short a time, as Mark Twain pointed out. This is a reconciliation of a natural and healthy conflict development, one that moved toward independence and mutuality.

The Gestalt psychologist Fritz Perls defines the therapeutic task in parental relationship as helping the client move from resentment to gratitude. Not everyone, however, makes this transition successfully. In a twisted personality the resentment can become strange and destructive. One wildly neurotic young man, known to the author, entered a hospital and had plastic surgery done on his navel so that he could remove the last vestige of his relationship with his mother. Another case involved a forty-one-year-old unmarried daughter who refused consent for her mother's life-saving surgery, arguing that it was too risky even though there was no hope of survival apart from the surgery. Her enfeebled eighty-eight-year-old mother finally revived sufficiently to sign the consent form herself.

Some parents, misunderstanding this fourth commandment's intention, have used it as a club to control their children's unruly behavior. The commandment does not enjoin children to obey unquestioningly. It does not force them to honor what is not honorable. It does not bless parental brutality or child abuse. It does not require submission to or toleration of unacceptable and inhuman behavior by parents toward children. We are called to honor in spite of and because of the life-forming intensity of the relationship that contributes most to the patterns of adult life. For good and for ill we are who we are as a result of the life we have received. In a real sense, then, honor to parents is honor to self.

For some the path to honor is arduous and soul crushing. When I was a young seminarian serving a congregation of tenant farm families in rural Virginia, one of my duties was to teach the Ten Commandments to a class of high-school students each Sunday morning. These children and teenagers were not well educated or sophisticated; they were simple, earthy people. When the exploration of "Honor your father and your mother" began, I became aware of the distress of one lovely blond girl, about fourteen, who was in the first blush of adult feminine beauty. Her beauty, however, was marred by an ugly scar across her forehead. Some years earlier her father had come home drunk and abusive one Saturday night and had split her head open when he kicked her down the stairs. The family did not seek medical attention. Perhaps they were too ignorant or too poor or too afraid of questions being asked. So the forehead was left to heal as best it could, with home remedies probably exaggerating the disfigurement.

The Christian Church is not called in the name of morality to lay upon this child the duty to accept the abuse and still honor her father. There is no honor in violence, in victimization, in drunkenness. This commandment must not be used to enforce childlike respect and obedience. That is not its focus. The commandment is a working principle designed to govern the obligation of adults to their elderly parents. It is not directed to children. In the life of this abused and scarred fourteen-year-old girl, "father" becomes a word that conjures feelings of fear and pain. Nevertheless, as an adult she must endure the memory and arrive at some kind of forgiveness for the man who is her father. That is not to say this cruel behavior should be excused. But it is to recognize that a parent will always be a major character in a child's life story. André Malraux has said, "One day it will be realized that human beings are distinguishable from one another as much by the forms their memories take as by their characters." It is also true that our characters are formed by the way we choose to remember our pasts. The abused childhood will continue to exert its tyranny in memory unless the battered child, now a woman, comes to terms with that abuse in a way that acknowledges its reality and then either sets it aside or transforms it to compassion for self and empathy for others who suffer similar pain and humiliation. She must do this for her own soul's health.

Children, like aged parents, have always been abused in significant numbers; we know that the weak and powerless receive the blows of rage and frustration that erupt when life's pressures exceed tolerance. Caring for children who necessarily demand time and attention requires considerable self-sacrifice. Just as it is more wish than reality that children always love their parents, so it is a misunderstanding of human personality to believe that parents instinctively love and desire to care for their offspring. Good parenting is learned most effectively by having been raised by loving parents or guardians. In order to grow into responsible, loving adults, we need the experience of different kinds of love and nurture. Fathers and mothers have played different roles in history, but both the feminine and the masculine forms of love are important.

It is very difficult in this age of new sensitivity to sexual discrimination to talk about the characteristics of feminine love and masculine love, for there is no assurance that one is accurately discerning a biological reality rather than a cultural role. But we can at least analyze the kinds of love that every child needs, and we can observe the ways that the culture has organized to provide that variety through primary care-givers of both sexes.

Apparently our humanity requires two distinct emotional responses. First, every one of us needs the security to be. We need love that is not discriminating, love that loves us just because we are, not because of what we do. We need a sense of belonging, a sense of community, an identity that no one can take away from us. Historically, this unconditional love has been expected from and assigned to the feminine figure, the mother image whose love is a graceful, nondemanding love based on the baby's being, not on the baby's doing. This archetypal mother love is given without distinction, simply because the baby is. This bond of love is indissoluble; nothing can destroy it. In order to be human we must build upon this security of being, this sense of belonging, this grace of acceptance by others. From this love one develops the ability to trust, the bedrock of human relationships.

But security alone does not produce mature humanity. Love that loves us because we are, love that does not challenge us, that demands no performance, results finally not in maturity but in a stunted, sick dependency. Hence, for the full power of human life to develop, there must be a second kind of love, one that historically the male has primarily supplied. This masculine love produces "the drive to become." The security to be must be coupled with the drive to become if one is to reach one's full human potential. This masculine love sets standards. It challenges, discriminates, rewards. In the masculine-dominated world of sports, for instance, the coach assigns positions on a team to those who win in competition. Masculine love drives one to achieve. It produces accomplishment, judgment, excellence. Love that fosters the drive to become is by definition not love that is equally shared among members of a family. Rather, it thrives on competition and is given to the one who most deserves it. In short, it is based not on being but on doing.

But just as love that produces the security to be is by itself inadequate, so love that produces the drive to become is by itself also inadequate. The drive to become, when separated from the security to be, creates not humanity but a jungle where might makes right, where the power to rule is the reward bestowed upon the aggressive super-achiever. Unchallenged, it would finally produce devastating domination and a rule of terror. Full, true humanity results from the delicate balance between the security to be and the drive to become. Both are essential to development of our humanity.

These qualities have been incorporated into our concepts of God. In the history of Western civilization at least, God has most often been pictured as masculine, addressed as "Father," and portrayed as a judge. This God is primarily the dispenser of rewards and punishments that we call heaven and hell, the distant giver of rules and commandments that set the standards that drive us to become. But this Father God has never existed alone. He is always seen working through the church which, interestingly, is called "Mother Church." To this divine ecclesiastical mother we belong equally at our baptism, which is not based on our doing but on our being, and in the bosom of this mother we are nurtured, fed, loved, "just as we are, without one plea." Here we are forgiven, accepted, and made secure to be—all of which enables us to be challenged by the Father God's will for us to become.

Is not the agenda that determines whether we are political conservatives or liberals related to these basic human needs, the security to be and the drive to become?

The political expression of the drive to become suggests that everyone should receive what he or she deserves, and nothing more. Those thus motivated tend to oppose welfare systems and governmental social security systems. They are typically individualistic and opposed to collectivization. These are the conservative principles. At the other end of the spectrum, the political expressions of the security to be suggest that everyone should be treated equally, that everyone should be cared for by the superparent—the government—from cradle to grave by a variety of security programs from Aid to Dependent Children to Medicare. These attitudes form the liberal principles that move toward a collectivization aimed at caring for all according to their needs alone.

Lest the reader think this far-fetched, consider that when the drive to become is unchallenged in the political arena, it appears as a right-wing fascism that is bound to have master-race implications. This political manifestation appeared in its most blatant form in Western civilization in a country known to its people as the "*Father*land." On the other hand, when the security to be is unchecked politically, it becomes a left-wing communal state that in its unadulterated form would take from each what that person has to give and give to each according to need. In the Western world the political manifestation of this attitude appeared as a state-enforced communism in the country known to its people as "*Mother* Russia."

Traditionally maternal love has produced in the recipient the security to be, and paternal love has produced the drive to become. Both are important and must be kept in tension, or humanity is at risk.

The fifth commandment expects that we will live as recipients of both kinds of love—those that give us both the security to be and the drive to become—which traditionally have been related to the roles of both parents, the mother and the father. For many people, social role continues to be assigned by gender, but psychologically each of us has feminine and masculine components within our personality. That means that we are able to love ourselves and others in a variety of ways and to honor all those who have cherished and encouraged us, to become the kinds of adults who can be parents for the next generation—the bearers of story and the transmitters of love. The span of individual life may be short, but the "braided cord" of generations will not be cut as long as we live within the inherited story of life and remain worthy of honor.

Chapter 9

THE SACREDNESS OF LIFE

"If freedom is the basis of all other human values, then there are times when men and women will have to choose between killing and surrendering their humanity."
—SAM KEEN

Contrary to our wishful thinking, we human beings are not peaceful, nonviolent creatures. Like other species, we have evolved into our present state. According to Charles Darwin's theory, the evolutionary process has been an intense struggle that only the strong and adaptable have survived. Force and cunning have been applied to survival issues that were economic at their base and, in fact, remain so. Developing Homo sapiens set themselves against the rest of the animal world to secure an adequate food supply, first by hunting (kill or be killed) and then, as civilization progressed, by domesticating animals. Wild edible grains and fruits gleaned along the hunting routes balanced the diet. As nomadic life gave way to a settled agrarian society, food-bearing vegetation was systematically planted, cultivated, and harvested. In both the settled and nomadic life, however, there was intense competition. In time of scarcity, aggressive tribes raided other tribes and seized their food by force to prevent starvation. Killing animals and fellow human beings to obtain food was frequent and expected. Competition has been woven into the fabric of human life from the beginning. Since the prize has been no less than life itself, the competition has gone on to the bitter end. To the victor have gone the treasures of the defeated. The instinct to fight or flee when confronted by threat is a life-saving impulse that remains a primary aspect in what we call human nature, although we may be unaware of its origin. Nor do we usually recognize it as a survival response.

We do not like to think of ourselves as being so connected to our primitive ancestors. We ignore the raw emotions that lie just beneath our thin layer of civilization. With rationalizations and compensating behaviors, we cover the springs of aggression that boil beneath our conscious minds. We have adopted saccharine attitudes and polite gestures as a way to manage our complicated world. But none of this changes the fact that we are prone to violence; we are jealous, competitive, and capable—even desirous—of hatred and killing. Our dark natures find vicarious release as our violence is portrayed realistically on television screens via the evening news, or in fantasy through Westerns, detective stories, police chronicles, and cartoons. Such mayhem would not entertain and titillate unless it was touching something deep within—something civilization will never completely suppress or eradicate.

It is no coincidence that one of the earliest stories in the biblical narrative is a tale of murder. The murder occurred not between strangers but between brothers. Cain murdered Abel in a jealous rage because his younger brother was the favored son. For that sin he was banished from the family and presumably lost his elder son's inheritance.

The story tells us what we all know but wish were not true. We cannot assume love between brothers and sisters in family life any more than can love between parents and children. Wishfully and sentimentally we love to talk about brotherly love. We even set aside a week each year to celebrate "brotherhood." Such a designation is as much longing as truth. In less secular generations, and with less sensitivity than we now have to women's concerns, the slogan of *brother*hood week was "the *brother*hood of man under the *father*hood of God." Beneath that shining banner we continue to wear the mask that hid Cain's murderous thought, if not his act. The more we deny the unacceptable thoughts and feelings that run counter to a parental training that promotes and tolerates peace at any price, the more likely it is that angry, jealous urges will slip out and catch us when we are not looking. Or else we project those images of hate and feelings of threat onto others, onto people who remind us of our early familial struggles. In this way we fashion our enemies from the discarded material of our own psyches.

We all remember the competition and rivalries of our childhood. When I was a boy, I of course loved my younger brother. I was constantly told I was supposed to, and so I said I did. But by some strange coincidence many accidents seemed to happen to him whenever we were alone together. We were playing on a seesaw once when we were quite young. I weighed more than he and was able to keep his end of the seesaw high off the ground. One day I kept him dangling there for so long that he decided to jump off. It certainly was not my fault that he broke his arm. Little kids ought not to jump from high places.

On another occasion some repairs were being made on our home. A few pieces of sawed lumber were scattered on the ground. I picked up a piece that had been cut to a sharp angle and threw it into the sky as high as I could. My little brother just happened to run exactly into the spot where it came down. That was certainly not my fault! He has an ugly scar in the top of his head today as a memento of his carelessness. Little kids ought to watch where they are going.

When I was twelve and he was nine, I decided it was his big brother's duty to teach him the manly art of self-defense. It was for his own good, I told him. We put on boxing gloves, and under the guise of a socially acceptable sport I gave him a broken nose and a deviated septum. Sometimes I think he is lucky to be alive. Nature and maturity eventually evened the odds. Today we are both adults, and not only do I respect and admire him, but he is 6 feet 4 inches tall and weighs 210 pounds.

The most personal experiences are also the most universal. It is within the family unit that human needs, both physical and emotional, are provided or withheld. Inevitably, mother's milk dries up and father does not praise enough. Blame falls on brothers and sisters with whom we must share parental attention. The certainty of resentment living side by side with affection and gratitude makes it doubtful that we will have the peaceful families that might lead to a peaceful world.

In an unsophisticated but accurate way the Hebrews observed the human personality, and though they did not call it by this name, they recognized sibling rivalry and its possible murderous consequences.

Excepting the first child, every child displaces the one immediately before it. No one likes to be displaced at any age; hostility and jealousy result from such dislocation. A desire to remove the intruder and to return to the less populated "garden" where one was the center of attention with little effort is the genesis of sibling rivalry. Sibling rivalry, an expression of our self-centeredness that inclines us away from sharing, never really abates. It changes targets, but it never disappears; so it is not surprising that civil wars are the bloodiest wars, for wars fought within the family always are bitter.

When he could not reconcile the unfairness of the father-god's preference for Abel's offering, Cain finally rose up and struck Abel dead in a blinding rage that anesthetized him against the affection and comradeship he might also have enjoyed. The emotions that precipitated that murder are in us, controlled and consigned to the place of forgetting, but escaping from time to time in unexpected and intemperate actions and words that are meant to hurt, to insult, to vindicate one's own position and ambition for power and status.

The Hebrew verb "to kill" used in this Exodus version of the commandment is spelled *rsh*. Though the verb appears in the Hebrew scriptures forty-six times, it is not easy to define. In some sense, "do not murder" is more accurate than "do not kill," for the law clearly accepted both killing in a war and execution by the proper authorities for some serious crimes against the community. Originally the law probably intended to forbid taking the law into one's own hands, lest a member of the community threaten its sanctity and security. The law protected against intratribal violence to ensure tribal survival, and it fostered identification with and loyalty to the tribal values. The context of the commandment, however, quickly expanded beyond tribal organizational needs. If a community views killing as wrong, it will be only a matter of time before categories such as justifiable homicides, legal executions, and just wars are instituted. By the time the Book of Numbers was written, the same verb for "to murder" is used to describe also a legal execution, and the exceptions to the commandment began to call forth legal commentary.

National traditions very quickly tempered the law. Cities of refuge were established to protect anyone who had killed unintentionally. Here one guilty of a murder that might be termed manslaughter could wait, safe from blood revenge, until the case could be heard. Vigilante justice was forbidden.

By the fifth century B.C.E., the priestly writer in the Book of Leviticus, with the religiously scrupulous in mind, had expanded the injunction against murder to include hating another in one's heart, even if the feeling was not acted upon. From this point it is easy to see that line of rabbinical thought reflected in Jesus' words in the Sermon on the Mount: "You have heard it said . . . , 'You shall not kill, and whoever kills shall be liable to judgment.' But I say to you that everyone who is angry with his brother shall be liable to judgment; whoever insults his brother shall be liable to the council" (Matthew 5:21–22). The literal intent of the commandment against murder became increasingly obscure. "You shall not kill" pointed to a hope for a better world that life and circumstances constantly reinterpreted. Through the years the Hebrew understandings of God and life were formed and re-formed, and the law was continually broadened and modified.

The Hebrew creation legend proclaimed that life had begun not just from the soil, the material of creation, but also from the animating, vitalizing breath of God. God breathed his *nephesh* into Adam. Only because of this was Adam "a living being." So were all the children of Adam, whether moral or immoral, male or female, slave or free, members of the clan or aliens. The seeds of universalism are found in the Hebrew attitude toward life. This attitude is also expressed in the sixth commandment, "You shall not kill."

The Hebrews were quick to act against practices in the ancient world that were common to other people but were abominations to their principle of the sacredness of life. Infanticide was prohibited in the Hebrew scriptures. Abandoning babies, especially female babies, was certainly not unusual even among the civilized Romans. To the Roman writer Tacitus, the Jewish prohibition against infanticide was a reason for anti-Semitism. On the other end of the lifeline, the Hebrews, holding fast to the sacredness of life, refused to dispatch their elderly to a certain death, as was acceptable in some other cultures.

The theme of sacred life is crucial to the biblical story and central to the complexities and moral dilemmas of the twentieth century. Because motive and deed could not easily be separated, not only the destructive acts that anger precipitated but the emotions that fed them came to be prohibited. Those distinctions remain in our courts, which differentiate between degrees of murder by deliberating accidental versus premeditated killings and the mental competence of the killer to distinguish between right and wrong. When the victims and killers were identifiable and the motivations are known or at least agreed upon, judgments can be made with a reasonable amount of confidence in the decision.

Those nuances seem quaint and enviously straightforward, compared to our current dilemmas. In this last quarter of the twentieth century we are facing ethical quandaries of life and death that spring not from scenes of interpersonal conflict but from the extraordinary escalations of technology. Fifty years ago young medical students heard their professors anticipate the advance of machines and medicines that would prolong life and create a whole new set of medical and moral dilemmas. That future is upon us. We can delay biological death with measures such as respirators, powerful chemotherapy, and organ transplants, and these measures no longer seem heroic since they are used so frequently. Experiments are being conducted to allow us to limit the application of laser-beam therapy to a single molecule. If this technique becomes practicable, cancer will be conquered and death could be pushed back significantly.

Ethical issues have turned from consideration of the preservation of life, to the quality of life, to the cost of resources—financial and human—and the proper allocation of these resources for the good of society. Does a terminal patient have the moral right to refuse treatment that would prolong life but not produce cure? At what point does technology interfere with death, an expected and normal part of life, rather than enhance life? I knew a man who committed suicide after he developed a particularly painful malignancy. All hope of cure was gone. To tolerate the pain would have required the addictive use of mind-depressing drugs. He chose to die by his own hand while still in control of his faculties. Did he cooperate with death, or interfere with life?

For those whose illnesses have moved them beyond an ability to take such initiative even if they wanted to, their predicaments appear on court dockets with requests for the removal of life-support systems, including forced feeding. Polls indicate that public opinion is more willing to accept the implications of new medical capabilities than are legislators, but the law of the land is gradually setting precedent after precedent on the side of not interfering with death when the quality of life is subhuman and the pain is intolerable.

To meet the new contingencies, medical centers have begun to bring professional ethicists onto their staffs. Hospitals commonly have ethics committees with representation drawn from practicing physicians, hospital administrators, clergy, the legal and nursing professions, and community leaders. Such committees develop policy, review records, and evaluate specific current cases. Life-and-death decisions are no longer individual matters. For too long, physicians have been placed in the untenable position of being the moral arbiters of medical ethics. Alone they took action that cast them in the role of saviors or executioners. One disastrous consequence of medical technology governed by physicians alone is the out-of-control litigation we have seen when things have gone wrong. Our confidence and insistence that all be well and that the promises of technology be kept for every individual have created a climate in which blame and retribution have fallen primarily on physicians and hospital administrators. As we wrestle with calamity, it is essential that as a society we both honor life and not deny death.

From the first moment of self-awareness human beings have carried the knowledge that death would come sooner or later, like a thief in the night, in accident or illness or by exposure to various other natural dangers. There was at least some comfort in not knowing the hour or the day of one's death. Now even that is changing. The hour is known when the respirator is removed, or when an elderly person with severe congestive heart failure is not revived. We know that life will end soon when an ethics board rejects a dialysis or transplant candidate or determines that a premature infant is too high a risk to mobilize the $300,000 effort that might be necessary to preserve its life. A death sentence is passed when surgery is withheld from a baby born with multiple incurable and life-threatening defects.

We continue to construct our definitions of life in terms of its quality and potential quality. We are also being forced to look at the economics of "life at any price," especially when those economic resources are available to the few rather than the many. We cannot continue to run our societal life on an emergency basis, responding to crisis and trauma with all available time, energy, and money, while chronic death-dealing life situations such as poverty, class and racial discrimination, and drug and alcohol abuse go on unabated. When considering the high costs of medical technology we become aware that the decisions to invest ourselves set priorities, since our resources are finite. Every yes has its corresponding no to some other concern or social problem or hurting individual. We cannot escape death, nor can we escape responsibility in decision making where a possible consequence is death. The sixth commandment is not an excuse for evading our responsibilities by designating as murderous all active interventions that hasten death or the intentional neglect that allows death. Because God has increasingly blessed us with memory, reason, and skill, and as we are made in the divine image, decisions of life and death are truly ours to make.

Beyond the medical emergencies of catastrophic illness there are four additional occasions of death to be explored in the light of "you shall not kill": suicide apart from terminal illness, abortion, war, and capital punishment.

Suicide

The Hebrews interpreted the sixth commandment as forbidding suicide. When suicide results from anger turned inward in an extreme expression of self-hatred and despair, it denies the holiness of life. Those who made their covenant with God did not consider the psychological dimension of this as we do, but they did understand that suicide is a fatal distortion of God's will for that life. The murder of self was a crime, and so it has been regarded in Judeo-Christian America where people unsuccessful in their suicide attempts were subject to arrest in some states until 1961, when the law was repealed. Out of the same attitude ecclesiastical (canon) law formerly denied Christian burial to suicides.

Very few suicides are recorded in the Hebrew or Christian scriptures. Saul fell on his sword after the Philistines had killed his sons in battle at Mount Gilboa and after all was lost. Ahithophel, Absalom's chief counsel, hanged himself when he lost face after his advice was rejected. The insurrectionist Zimri reigned as king of Israel for seven days and died in a fire he set in the palace when he was about to be overthrown. Judas hanged himself, according to the gospel of Matthew, after his betrayal of Jesus. These were overt cases of the conventional understanding of suicide. But there are others less obvious, less traditional.

The church has not always regarded all suicide as sin. In the early centuries of Christianity, with the church reeling under heavy persecution, church leaders rewarded martyrs by encouraging the faithful not to recant. Tertullian, a second-century church father, wrote, "The blood of the martyrs is the seed of the church." A doctrine developed that promised immediate entrance into heaven without any side trips through purgatory for all those who gave their lives for the church. The overly zealous provoked arrest that their souls might be assuredly redeemed. Religious extremists of other religions, then as now, have used the same promise of an eternal reward to achieve both political and religious ends. It was true of Japanese kamikaze pilots in World War II and of Buddhist monks in Vietnam, and it is true of Islamic terrorists in our day. It was a major force in the life of the early Christians. Yet that behavior is clearly suicidal.

A third motivation for suicide is a desire to bring about a greater good. In this category we might list Samson's destruction of the temple, in which he was killed. Even Jesus could have avoided Jerusalem and a probable execution had he not been a man with a mission. History is filled with protestors who publicized their cause and tried to elicit support for the sake of justice by taking their own lives through fasting or provoking execution. Those whose causes we shared we called martyrs, witnesses to the good. But they were suicides nonetheless. Who among us is today ready to give a simplistic moral judgment on so complex a human activity?

Abortion

Abortion is particularly interesting to discuss at this point, for it is pivotal to the discussion on sexuality that follows in the chapter on the seventh commandment, which forbids adultery. The connections of sex to sin are tangential to both prohibitions.

We already know that taking life or being an accomplice to such an action is not always an immoral act. Certain acts of euthanasia and suicide are not regarded as either crime or sin. In those cases where killing is removed from the category of sin, it has had the consequence either of enhancing life or of curtailing a lingering, painful, inevitable death. Quality of life has been a measure in the moral judgment; therefore some areas of discussion on abortion are simply inappropriate to the topic. There is no point in attempting to determine a time in the life of the fetus when life "begins" or when the fetus becomes a "person." Let us just agree that we are dealing with life—mother and child—and with potential life—mother and child, and in cases where parental responsibility is truly shared, mother, father, and child. The commandment calls us to honor life as it is and as it can be within the mind of God. No discussion of the morality of abortion can be accomplished apart from the consequences, the future implications of the decision for or against abortion.

We cannot discuss abortion apart from considering better methods of birth control, including male contraceptives that would be the modern equivalent to those developed for women in the last three decades. The issue of abortion is intrinsically connected to the care and nurture of children who are born when a pregnancy goes to term. That means we need residential homes for single, pregnant women who want to keep their babies and who need to know parenting skills. Presently, most such homes are really adoption agencies that require the baby as payment for services rendered. We desperately need reasonable day-care facilities so that children of parents who work are not left alone to raise themselves as best they can. We need required sex education in schools, including information on contraceptives. We cannot consider death and murder except as they relate to life.

If the legal and moral stance of the community prohibits all abortion, then the quality of the life of both mother and child, as well as of all whose lives intersect theirs, may well be diminished even to the point of death. The deterioration of mental and physical health in those who are forced to seek illegal abortions or to bear unwanted children is astonishing. The consequences of anti-abortion laws as a whole turn away from the sanctity of life and so contribute to the decay of society. Given our current social attitudes and low level of economic commitment to children and their parents, abortion on request becomes a responsible recourse. It is time to turn more of our resources and our concern for life to the children who are already born and who need our help.

At the moment, abortion requests are made by individuals, but the number of humans being born is increasingly a communal concern. It is not inconceivable that overcrowding and limited resources may bring a state mandate limiting the number of children per family, as is now the case in China. Should overpopulation threaten the very survival of the human race, abortion as a moral question will gather dust in the archives of social history.

Abortion is a major issue today in the discussions revolving around the place of women in society. For most of human history, biology has been destiny in the lives of women. Woman's role as outlined in Genesis 3 was to be dependent on her husband and to bear children in pain. As the one who took initiative in the garden scene, woman has been regarded not only as "the mother of all living" but as the mother of sin as well, and therefore deserving of punishment. While there has been no moral outrage at Adam's descendants' relinquishing their God-given role as farmers (see Genesis 3), women have not had many options until now. In part, assent to abortion is assent to woman's changing destiny and "forgiving" her (sexual) sins. Centuries of entrenched negative mythology about women's place and punishment unconsciously send tendrils throughout any sexual issue.

Before turning to the commandment that specifically addresses sexuality, we must consider two more arenas of death. Both of these deal with death by community action rather than by individual decision, and so are all the more difficult to engage.

War

For the first time in human history we have the power to destroy all life on earth. Considerations of a just or unjust, moral or immoral, war recede against the specter of a nuclear holocaust that haunts the world with increasing probability. In the context of such potential annihilation, there is no real debate. Anything other than unilateral nuclear disarmament is a death strategy. Even those who call for bilateral nuclear freeze and mutual nuclear disarmament, who ask our government to renounce publicly the possibility that this nation will ever use nuclear weapons in a first strike, see the moral dimensions of this overwhelming danger, but they are not moved to action appropriate to that danger.

This position of nuclear pacificism is born of the belief that deterrence through fear is contrary to the gospel. We are called to love, not hate. We can no longer be willing to be bound by the ancient tribal mentality that tells us whom to hate and who our enemies shall be. Surely there are citizens like us in communist countries—people who also do not accept the propaganda of their governments and who are now ready to stand and be counted. The madness of the world's political leadership that entertains nuclear war as a possible means of achieving national aims must be confronted by the unarmed power of the concerned citizenry.

The requirement to love one's neighbor, accepted at Sinai, made Israel's wars of self-defense and conquest increasingly untenable. Day by day and century by century, God has led the people of the covenant into an expanding awareness of community until now every person on this tiny planet qualifies as our neighbor. In such a world the very planning of nuclear war is immoral; stockpiling of nuclear weapons keeps us slaves to our own fear. Many call this position "naive, unrealistic, and typical of religious mentality dealing with an intricate political question." But here we must declare crusades for our own soul's sake and for the sake of liberty as God would give it to us. Proponents of peace often appear foolish, but the foolishness of the pacifist is not nearly so foolish as the insanity that marks those who, in a nuclear age, act as if war were still a viable option.

Capital Punishment

Community life-and-death issues defy consensus. Just as there are many minds about nuclear disarmament, so there are diverse opinions about capital punishment. As citizens and Christians we must take our individual stands and not let those community decisions be made by default. Unlike nuclear war, which is a unique moral question not possible before this generation, state execution has been a prominent part of the organization of human life throughout recorded history.

The Bible certainly permits and legislates executions, but we cannot use biblical precedents to support capital punishment unless we select our texts very carefully. In scripture, death is prescribed as the punishment for numerous crimes, including murder, treason, kidnapping, idolatry, blasphemy, false prophecy, witchcraft, being an incorrigible adolescent, breaking the sabbath, rape, adultery, incest, sexual perversion, uttering a curse, striking a parent, and bearing false witness in a death-penalty trial. Few would be willing to consider this biblical list as acceptable reasons for executions today. Even in the Bible, as soon as capital crimes were defined, the Hebrew sense of the sacredness of life began to moderate the punishment and thereby made the death penalty harder and harder to exact, just as we have done today. If the accused confessed, execution was forbidden. Death could not be exacted on circumstantial evidence alone; two witnesses had to agree that a murder was deliberate, that the act was premeditated, and that the killer was warned but did not heed the warning. Finally, the witnesses had to be willing to act as the state's executioners.

In those ways the spirit overcame the letter of the law. It is that same spirit that leads us to assert that the death penalty should be banned where it is still practiced and not be revived where it has been banned. A civilized society must deter criminal elements, but it does not need to take revenge. There is no evidence that the death penalty deters capital crimes. If deterrence cannot be served by capital punishment, then revenge is the only rational explanation for its continued practice. This is simply not an acceptable pattern of behavior for a just and humane society.

State execution brutalizes life. It fails to recognize society's corporate responsibility for the distortions that appear in any one of society's children. The death penalty falls heaviest on the poor and the illiterate, both of whom have limited resources and limited access to adequate legal representation. And there is always the risk of executing the innocent.

I was once a prison chaplain on death row, with the responsibility of ministering to an inmate who was later executed. Everything about his execution was brutal. It was life-denying, vengeful, and dehumanizing—life at its very worst. It repels me even today to recall it. "You shall not kill" is a demand upon the state as well as upon the individual.

Life imprisonment is an alternative with many negative consequences. Prisons brutalize guards as well as inmates. The very act of keeping prisoners draws the keepers into a dehumanizing pattern until jailer and the jailed are sometimes indistinguishable. Yet prisons are still the only method society has developed to isolate criminals from their potential victims. The victims of crime merit our concern, but the issues of deterrence and public safety need to reflect the highest ideals of the society, not the lowest. Those issues are not well served when politicians play on the fears of people to gain support. It is easy to campaign against crime and criminals; it is difficult to take the necessary actions that will get at the root causes of crime.

Some years ago, at an annual Brotherhood Awards dinner of the National Conference of Christians and Jews, the governor of the host state was the speaker. Unfortunately, he used this occasion to indulge in inflammatory political oratory, calling on his audience to "get the criminal element and give them what they deserve." The dinner guests enthusiastically applauded just before awards were presented to those who had contributed most to the ideal of brotherhood in that community that year. The incongruity was obvious but publicly unrecognized.

The Hebrews would have felt the disjointedness of those moments, for the commandment not to kill was more than a law to curb jealousy and hatred, though that was important; it was also a call to live out a new humanity not ruled by envy, jealousy, or hostility.

"You shall not kill" finally turns into a positive command. You shall give life. You shall live in such a way as to be creators of a world where the quality of life is an equal or greater value than the quantity of life. God's call to celebrate and enhance life accompanies and interprets the demands of the covenant. From the perspective of the Christian life, Jesus appears as both the giver and keeper of the law. He was so alive to the reality of God, so transparent to the love of God, so at one with the life of God that Christians assert that God was the center of his being. All the human bitterness, rivalry, jealousy, envy, and human hostility were transformed in this Christ into a life-giving power that absorbed abuse, endured pain, allowed death, and gave only love in return. This was the full response to the covenant, and that is why Christians see in Jesus the human face of the invisible God. In that human life the final paradoxical meaning of the sixth commandment is made evident. The victim dead upon the cross was strangely alive and life-giving, while the executioners who gazed upon that lifeless body did not seem to recognize that they were the ones who were dead. It is the contrary logic of biblical truth that death and life masquerade as each other. It is therefore not enough to obey the letter of the law; one must also feel the spirit of the law's intention. That spirit calls us first to live life and then to share life, without counting the cost.

Chapter 10

BODIES AND RELATIONSHIPS

"Christianity gave Eros poison to drink—he did not die of it, to be
sure, but degenerated into vice."   —FRIEDRICH NIETZSCHE

"Happy families are all alike; every unhappy family is
unhappy in its own way." With this opening line of *Anna Karenina,* Leo
Tolstoy engages the reader by eliciting a sign of recognition. Though
we may have desperately wanted to believe that Cinderella and her
prince really did "live happily ever after," disenchantment usually
sets in during the second year of marriage, when the eyes of the recently
married are opened to the realization that people who make commitments to intimate, sexual relationships become vulnerable to suffering
and pain as well as to pleasure and ecstasy. We cannot know or be
known without being thwarted and disappointed sooner or later.

Tolstoy's heroine entered into a marriage with an older man who
gave her economic security and social position but who was emotionally distant, domineering, and finally cruel. When Anna scandalized everyone by leaving her husband for another man, her ostra-
cism by the community was complete. Tolstoy, who converted to
radical Christianity in his adult years, wrote moral tales whose
endings were predictable. Sinners were punished; adulteresses came
to a bad end. The tales were told, however, in a way that left the
impression that the suffering sinner had been curiously victorious at
the last. Shunned and unable to reset the course of her life, Anna threw
herself under the wheels of a train. The story concluded with the
tragedy of a life ended by despair, but throughout the narrative there
was also the continuous spark of courage and the untamed passion for
life that bore Anna into the adulterous relationship in which she felt
fully alive, able to love and be loved. In spite of her suicide, she was a
woman without regret. Anna Karenina risked and lost . . . and won.

In literature and in life, sex is a complex, paradoxical, and emotionally charged subject. We know its power both to tarnish and to

brighten relationships. Some engage in it in healthy, life-enhancing ways. For such people, sex is woven into life's tapestry. It threads its way throughout, coloring all behavior, impossible either to ignore or to push aside. Each of us is not just a human being. We are either a human male or a human female, driven to reproduce ourselves. Our yearning for union is emotional and spiritual as well as biological, for we long for companionship as well as progeny. Sex is of creation, the Bible asserts, and as a component of human life it is good. There are many ways to express our sexuality. We can enjoy, savor, discipline, repress, or even redirect it. We cannot, however, deny it without significant consequences.

At the same time, we know that sex misused and misdirected leads to a diminishing of life, even to death. In particular we know the debilitating and damaging private and public consequences of illicit and furtive sex. In families and societies where sex is a taboo subject, it assumes the characteristics of an exotic creature such as a lobster or a poisonous snake that is both dangerous and fascinating. Sex as a creature in a glass cage is at the core of pronography. The observer is thrilled without the dangers of physical contact and the demands of relationship. The bewitching fear resulting from an ambivalent sexual attitude encourages obsessive actions and counteractions that interfere with the normal progress of daily life and become emotionally debilitating. When the pain does not go away, people often look for help from friends, pastors, and professional counselors. Wide varieties of sexual problems, under many guises and forms, cripple functioning. In the course of a typical pastorate, clergy encounter heterosexual and homosexual problems in both males and females: unresponsiveness and insatiable desire, premarital pregnancies, and postmarital childlessness. People come for counsel with problems connected to fetishes, perversions, rape, incest, infidelity, romantic attachments, affairs across racial lines, family lines, and generation lines. Life comes through the pastor's door exposed.

Sensitive pastors and friends, informed by the Christian value system, first love, accept, and forgive people where they are at the moment, and then encourage the kinds of changes that are self-restoring. An uncritical application of moral precepts and rigid rules to hurting lives trapped in a compromised society is not righteousness. It is lovelessness. Laws made for the good of the whole society have little relevance to individuals whose personal histories force them to make choices not from ideal options but from available ones. No one ever sins alone. Sin occurs in the company of others, where our choices affect one another. It is the human lot both to inherit the sins of past generations and to be aware of those determining factors as well. Unless one is willing to return to the society and era that marked the exile people of Sinai, where individualism is not yet formed and identity is found solely in the community mind, then there must always be individual exceptions to general rules. The complicated contingencies of a unique life situation cannot be measured by a single moral yardstick without sacrificing love.

In the last half-century new truths and new attitudes have fueled a sexual reformation. Standards, values, and choices are being redefined and altered. The task of the Christian in such a world is not well served by remaining ignorant of or blind to these changes. The seventh commandment and the axioms that have governed sexual behavior are still relevant in topic, if not always in interpretation. The delineation between sexual morality and immorality has become more fluid as we search for ourselves as sexual beings who are free to be wholly ourselves in relationship to another but without abrogating our responsibility to society.

This generation must find a place between the cultural and religious sexual ethics of yesterday, which encouraged repression, and the hedonistic sexual ethics of many people today, which suggest that "if you enjoy it, it must be good." Repression surfaces as paralyzing guilt and inhibition; the pleasure principle dissipates sexuality and prevents commitment. Surely there is another alternative.

The dynamic motivating power of sex has biological and psychological dimensions as well as moral ones. A refusal to discuss sex out of fear of contaminating the mind or from a misguided delicacy is a naive, not a moral, stance. Cognizance of new insights into human sexuality from the life sciences does not, as some religious critics complain, contribute to the breakdown of morality. Knowledge is amoral; as a tool it can be used for good or for ill. It is we who are culpable, not the agents that serve us. Sexual information can help us develop a moral code that is in touch with both our traditional Christian convictions and the information breakthroughs of this age. Repression will no longer keep the genie of sex bottled, nor will permissiveness diminish its mysterious power. Whether one accepts, rejects, welcomes, or dreads change, yesterday's repressive patterns do not govern or control public sexual attitudes or private sexual behavior today. Indeed, a careful reading of history shows that over the centuries, cultural expectations have exerted far less control over private sexual behavior than moralists would have us believe.

Because it is so easy to confuse religious principles with societal norms, Judeo-Christian principles need to be separated from the cultural accretions of time.

The original prohibition against adulterous relationships came from a people who continued to practice polygamy for many years after their covenant at Sinai. Monogamous marriage is not the original context of the injunction. This commandment was presumed to have been given in the wilderness around the year 1250 B.C.E. Yet 300 years later Solomon, with his 300 wives and 700 concubines, reigned as king in a land whose law proclaimed, "You shall not commit adultery."

The patriarchal society in which this law was both interpreted and applied did not regard sexual intercourse between a married man and an unmarried woman as an adulterous offense. A story in Chapter 38 of Genesis told of Judah's affair with Hirah, an Adullamite who was described only as his friend, even after he had had three children by her. In Chapter 21 of Judges, the men of Benjamin seduced first and married second. A man was found guilty of adultery only if he took another man's wife. Adultery was primarily an offense against another's man's marriage, not against his own. A married woman, on the other hand, committed adultery if she had a sexual liaison with any man. If a married man avoided married women, he could have as many sexual affairs as he wished and still not violate this commandment. Indeed, in the biblical law the seduction of a man's unbetrothed daughter was regarded as an offense against his property, not as a transgression of the seventh commandment.

Adultery, thus defined, was also an offense against the community, for marriage has never been just a private relationship. Marriage in the biblical period was arranged and approved by the family. Romance was not a consideration. Family property and political alliances were major concerns. Blood lines, family ties, and inheritances were matters of great importance. The conservation of wealth, and care in genetic selection through the choice of a mate, were means of keeping the tribe strong and untainted. As every act of intercourse with a fertile woman made pregnancy possible, there could be no assurance about the paternity of children unless women were sexually faithful. The keeping of the law also protected married women against demanding males, who would have been difficult to resist in a patriarchal society, and so contributed to the ordered life of the nation.

Though the seventh commandment did not apply to unmarried daughters, as potential wives their virginity was a valuable commodity. A deflowered virgin might have remained in her father's house as an expensive and less productive member of society than if she had married. If her honor were compromised, her seducer was expected to marry her. If he refused, he was required to pay her family the bride's price. She might then be married off to a less desirable mate. Unmarried and barren women carried enormous shame for having failed their duty and destiny as women. Such intolerable lives were regarded as reproaches from the Lord.

Women in this society needed the protection of a male—husband or kin—to survive. Though the commandment appeared to give men sexual license, society's organization inhibited licentiousness. Polygamy provided for excess women in a world where war and accidents killed off men and left women defenseless. There were continual reminders in the scriptures to care for the widows and orphans.

Female partners for men outside of marriage were unfortunate women who had no kin to provide a home for them. Prostitution was, and is, often a response to economic necessity. There was probably very little consensual "free" sex within the community. Sexual behavior with foreign women encountered while traveling or captured in war, however, was not governed by these laws. Therefore, the only sexual relations that were sufficiently disrupting to the community to occasion a prohibition were those that threatened the family structure upon which the survival of the entire community rested. Out of biological necessity, women were the inviolate guardians of the family treasures: children, inheritance, and political alliance.

Now, within the narrow scope of definition that regulated tribal inheritance, adultery—that is, sex by a man with someone else's wife, or sex by a married woman with any man other than her husband—was condemned, and the guilty person could be sentenced to death.

The Hebrew word for adultery used in this commandment was *na'aph,* a word that could apply to either a man or a woman.

Though the sin of adultery and its consequences were clearly stated, the sin was not a result of the negative, repressive attitude toward sex that is a trait of moralistic legalism today and that clearly is not biblical. There was no Jewish Queen Victoria. There was no disgust about the body or exaltation of the soul in Hebrew thought. That came from another tradition. The Hebrews were a lusty, life-affirming people; their literature reveled in the celebration of life.

Some years ago I taught a Bible class that was broadcast over a local radio station each Sunday. On one occasion the station managers "bleeped" my program because in their judgment the words being used were offensive to their listeners' ears. Much to the station managements' surprise and chagrin, they discovered that what they had censored was a passage read verbatim from the Bible. (The King James version at that!) My text—The Song of Songs—was a series of love poems that explicity extolled the physical beauty of a woman's body.

Thy lips are like a thread of scarlet. . . . Thy temples are like a piece of pomegranate within thy locks. They neck is like the tower of David. . . . Thy two breasts are like two roes which feed among the lilies . . . How fair is thy love, my spouse. How much better is thy love than wine and the smell of thine ointments than all spices. Thy lips drop as the honeycomb. Honey and milk are under thy tongue. . . . Open to me, my love, for my head is filled with dew and my locks with the drops of the night (Song of Songs 4:3 ff and 5:26 KJV).

The bridegroom's poems in Chapters 4 and 5 of the Song of Songs capture much of the Hebrew attitude toward bodies, toward sexuality, toward the beauty of the feminine form. The poems are no less lyrical about the bride's desire for her betrothed. These words are not read often in church are are even less often used as texts for sermons, except when allegorized in a wild and irrelevant exegetical exercise. They appear in the lectionary only as optional readings for marriages.

The antibody, antisex attitude that equates sexual intercourse with defilement and exalts virginity as the highest vocation is not now and never has been Hebraic.

When conventional religious attitudes are separated from the Judeo-Christian revelation, we begin to understand that the repressive moralism against which our culture has been in such rebellion is not necessarily Christian or biblical at all. Repressive moralism is a product of the dualistic Greek mind, which tended to devalue the physical and material as less worthy than the nonphysical or spiritual. This dualism reached its zenith in Western civilization when it combined with a puritan zeal to remove beauty and merriment from life. "If it's fun, it must be sinful!" Christianity was identified with a strict moralism and a rigid austerity. The nineteenth-century Victorian age followed with an increased appreciation for material comforts but a continuation of sexual restraints as the unquestioned rule of the day, at least in "proper" society. Absence of interest in sex was, in fact, a mark of good breeding for the women of that generation. Mothers advised brides to "lie there and think of England."

This attitude that made a virtue out of sexual denial was adopted by moralistic Christianity to become the powerful, controlling superstructure that held the sexual drives of human beings in check. The denial of sexual pleasure as a human good was accomplished by identifying sex with base, animal instinct and evil. The longstanding interpretation of the Garden disobedience as a result of Eve's success in enticing Adam to sin through her sexual seduction continued to play its part in the marriage bed. The purpose of sex was procreation, not shared pleasure. If sex was not enjoyed, it was less sinful. The pain of childbirth was punishment for sin, according to the myth of Eden. Long after anesthesia was invented, its analgesic effect was denied to women in labor since the Bible related the pain of childbirth to the woman's punishment for her sin. Queen Victoria ended that cruelty by using anesthesia to ease her own labors and then publicizing its relief.

The combination of sexual prejudice and the actual dangers of pregnancy and disease successfully repressed normal desire and rendered sex an unholy activity save for the single purpose of procreation. This denial created guilt about natural feelings and set the stage for a rebellion led by Sigmund Freud, who postulated that all human behavior was undergirded and motivated by sexual impulses. His insistence that sexuality pervaded behavior from birth scandalized his turn-of-the-century world. It was unthinkable in that day to regard innocent children as so tainted. Everyone "knew" that the corruption of sexuality came upon one in puberty. William Wordsworth spoke for that attitude when he wrote, "The child is father of the man," meaning that the innocence of childhood is closer to God and that there is a holy wisdom in that innocence. Though Freud eventually overstated his theories on sexuality, giving them absolute authority in his understanding of behavior, he nevertheless challenged sexual assumptions with clinical data that were difficult to refute.

Two world wars shattered the organized patterns of society by establishing new, temporary priorities that broke open the repressive sexual codes.

It may have been that the needs of society during the preceding century called for rigidity in sexual morals. Perhaps the Victorian age could not have managed in any other way to preserve the orderliness of life, the advance of civilization, the protection of the family, the control of disease, and the ethics of a culture that had become highly individualized. Sexual repression also served to convert sexual energy to other pursuits. The industrialization of England and America was accomplished during that time of rigid behavioral constraints. Bodily passions were submerged to an unconscious level, from which they reentered common life through the arts. Painting, music, interior design with its velvet, fringes, and sculptured ornamentation engaged the senses with a voluptuous sensuality that was discouraged in proper personal relationships.

Social and religious pressures worked in concert to keep the delicate balance of an ordered and progressive population. Childbirth out of wedlock was an unspeakable disgrace to a family and a blemish on the unwed mother and her child for life. A sexual profligate was assured of hell, said the church. Some religious orders still exclude those born on "the wrong side of the blanket" from high positions of leadership.

Social diseases, virulent and fearful, were regarded as nothing less than divine retribution for sin. A limerick popular at that time went like this:

> There was a young lady named Wilde
> Who kept herself quite undefiled
> By thinking of Jesus
> and social diseases
> And the fear of having a child.

The triple terrors of "detection, conception, and infection" fostered sexual inhibition. An effective chaperon system was developed to ensure virginity. Public opinion and religious attitudes combined to make sexual expression, save in the context of marriage, the worst of all possible sins and the major area of moral concern. In eighteenth-century puritan America, adultery was punishable by death, while child-beating and wife-beating were considered only unfortunate. No one stopped to examine whether such a moral position was true to our biblical heritage. Tradition moved those sexual attitudes into Christian doctrine. Nathaniel Hawthorne's brilliant nineteenth-century portrayal of an unwed mother, Hester Prynne, in *The Scarlet Letter* illustrated both the rigid morality of the Christian community and the true nature of sin that is untouched by moral law: those who condemn are also among the guilty.

It is interesting to note that Jesus had nothing to say in any of the four gospels about such things as sexual mores in courtship. Wherever we have very clear rules about that, they cannot be rooted in the Christian gospel itself.

Similarly, Jesus had nothing to say about sexual perversion. Nor did he comment on masturbation, reproduction, birth control, or abortion. Our training and education on these subjects evolve from tradition. This is not to say that the tradition is in error; it is only to say there is no biblical word from Jesus that authoritatively places each of these momentous issues into a right and wrong category, even for Christians.

Though we have no record that Jesus was ever married, we do know that he is never quoted as supporting celibacy. The gospels portray him as enjoying the company of women and attending parties and weddings. The symbol of marriage was central to a number of his parables. At times he referred to himself as "the bridegroom." Nothing antiphysical or antisexual appeared in the gospels. Legalistic moralism cannot be identified with first-century Judeo-Christian attitudes on sex. It was rather a product of historical evolution as people struggled to combine their understanding of sex, their value systems, and the circumstances of their lives. It is not our task to be critical of or to condemn their conclusions so much as it is to understand why our ancestors chose to deal with sexuality in that particular way.

As time advances and knowledge increases, however, the way we deal with the changes and chances of life must vary accordingly. In this century the circumstances surrounding sex and the perceptions of sexuality itself have been modified. The attitudes of the past assume circumstances that no longer exist and so have become irrelevant.

Four major transformations affect sexual behavior in the twentieth-century. First, sex and procreation are no longer necessarily linked. Confidence in reliable birth-control measures has separated lovemaking from baby-making. As a result, the sexual prohibitions designed to prevent illegitimate births no longer possess the same urgency. Additionally, increased longevity has enabled sexually active older couples to have many non-childbearing years together; this makes it obvious that sex and childbearing are no longer fused.

Secondly, the age of puberty has dropped. One hundred years ago, the average age of puberty in both sexes was sixteen or seventeen. Marriage, particularly of girls (at least in the dominant strata of society that set the norms), generally took place one or two years after puberty. Today, puberty takes place at age eleven or twelve, and marriage somewhere between twenty-one and thirty. How "natural" is sexual abstinence from puberty to marriage in such a long, culturally imposed separation? What is the emotional and physical price that virginity requires in this kind of world, and are we prepared to pay it? These issues must be weighed by those who would set moral standards.

Thirdly, in the highly mobile culture of the automobile, the chaperon system of a century ago is impossible. Whenever external controls are diminished, the alternative is to build internal controls to protect one's "honor" and "virtue." If these self-regulated internal controls become too fixed, the price in physical and emotional health is costly. Marriage may not turn off these rigid mental controls; if they remain, they can create a host of common problems that no one regards as desirable.

The fourth great change is in the status of women, who are now educated with men at the same schools and who have entered the economic marketplace as peers in medicine, finance, law, business, and professional ministry. Today's woman has the same freedom and opportunity that enabled her mobile male counterpart in previous generations to experiment and test relationships, some of which may have a sexual component. The double standard in sexual morality is disappearing.

One deterrent that remains is the powerful fear of infection, a fear that formerly inhibited sexual activity. Through the middle decades of this century there was an optimistic reliance on miracle drugs to control venereal disease. In previous eras sexually transmitted diseases were devastating in their effect, producing sterility, abscesses, brain damage, mental illness, and death. The premature confidence that such diseases could be controlled, or even eradicated, faded as the offending bacteria developed super strains that were impervious to existing drugs. Indiscriminate sexual behavior incubated and spread numerous sexually transmitted viruses, the most lethal of which is acquired immune deficiency syndrome (AIDS), and for which there is at this writing no cure or means of pharmaceutical prevention. This fact continues to act as an inhibitor of sexual behavior.

We live in a new century in which procreation has been separated from sexual activity, the time between puberty and marriage has been stretched to ten years or more, the chaperon system has been discarded, and women have claimed new roles. These changes have rendered the repressive superstructure of yesterday inoperable; and, like Humpty Dumpty, all the king's horses and all the king's men will never put it together again.

These are the issues that have forced new questions into our conscious minds. They are questions that a previous generation would not have asked and this generation is not yet able to answer. What is the basis for sexual morality for Christians in this age? Is there an area between the ideal and the immoral where sexual relations between consenting unmarried adults could be viewed in some way other than as destructive or wrong? Can the Christian church look at such relationships without naysaying judgment? Can we understand even if we do not fully approve? Can sexual activity apart from the context of marriage ever be more positive than negative? Can it in some conceivable set of circumstances contribute to life more than it erodes life? Is abstinence the only choice a Christian ethic can tolerate for widows, widowers, unmarried adults, or divorced people? Without intending to suggest that we can supply the answers, we will attempt to address those questions.

There must be self-consciously chosen guidelines that arise out of our living covenant that we can find to direct us to some appropriate ethical stance for our generation. If there is not, our destiny is to drift into new patterns of behavior without thinking. That stance may well be what many would consider short of perfection. It cannot, however, be simply a variation of yesterday's repressive system, for that will not win today's world. How can the commandment "You shall not commit adultery" be approached within the actualities of the twentieth century? Even more importantly, how can we help our children, who face complex sexual decisions to make life-affirming choices? How can character and commitment be strengthened, and repression and manipulation be opposed? How can the religious respect for stabilizing tradition be balanced against the call to become our true selves in the image of God? Between these life tensions, Christian ethics are formed.

In the pastoral ministries of the authors, nondefinitive guidelines have emerged that have helped some who try to follow a path of good when right and wrong categories seem not to apply. These guidelines are grounded in the Christian revelation, and together they provide a framework for making decisions about sex.

First, sex as a good gift to human life is best expressed within a relationship through which it will communicate both the holiness of life and the gratification of sexual desire.

Second, the holiness of life and the gratification of desire cannot be separated without causing dehumanization.

Third, sexual behavior and sexual expressions must be in harmony with natural biological development or sexual expressions will become distorted. The delay of sexual activity by more than a decade beyond the time of puberty creates an unnatural forced abstinence that is biologically abnormal.

Fourth, marriage is sacred. Fidelity to the marriage vows is an essential ingredient in the development of personality, the functioning of parenthood, and the stability of society. Unfaithfulness in marriage runs the risk of diminished life. Only in the most unusual circumstances could such sexual infidelity ever be justified. The reasons must be more compelling than boredom. There is no normal biological urge in any human being that cannot be satisfied inside the sexual exclusiveness of marriage. There is no biological necessity for a variety of sexual partners. Nothing but the human ego is involved in the incessant desire for new thrills and new conquests, which are designed to overcome one's own psychological doubts and fears.

Fifth, the Christian ethic is not rooted in sexual abstinence. It is rooted in the celebration of life. Sexual indiscretions are not the most profound transgressions, but they are moral breaches. Sexual prohibitions are always intended to enable something of great value to be achieved. Sometimes, however, sexual prohibitions violate life and form patterns of distortion. When such a time comes, the prohibition needs to be set aside. Virginity has a value, especially in the young, but if virginity can be achieved only by suppressing and distorting the good and wondrous gift of sexual expression; if virginity can be maintained only by surrounding sex with guilt and fear; or if virginity builds protective habits of mind and behavior that wedding bells do not automatically reverse, then the price of virginity has become too high.

Just as there may be consequences for coercive abstinence, so there are consequences attached to a decision for sexual activity. Parents need to teach and encourage responsibility in all decision making. Pregnancy and sexually transmitted diseases are possible consequences of intercourse. Disease prevention and contraception are appropriate topics of conversation between parents and adolescent children. Parental reluctance is understandable; education can be confused with permission giving. However, silence is no protector of behavior. Though females have historically been the keepers of mores, male as well female must share responsibility for sexual conduct. Sexual education is every bit as important for sons as it is for daughters.

Sexual dialogue between parents and children is necessary not only as a preventative against disease and unwanted pregnancy but also as preparation for intimacy. Sex between two people is an expression of intimacy. The goal of relationship is intimacy, not sexual fulfillment. It is possible to truncate a relationship by introducing a sexual component too soon. There are times when a developing relationship is derailed by sexual involvement that replaces courtship, a process that takes in other people and calls for verbal and nonsexual sharing of experiences. The incandescent quality of sexual passion quickly consumes a relationship that has laid no foundation for an enduring commitment. Many a budding friendship has been sacrificed to ignited emotions that burn out in a shallow bed. Many a tenuous commitment could not withstand the vulnerability and self-exposure that accompanies sexual intimacy. We can neither give nor receive nakedness until a base of care and understanding is established. Sex is rarely a shortcut to deepening a relationship, though it often pretends to be just that.

There is wisdom in the rules that confine sex to marriage, not only for the sake of societal order, but for the sake of the individual as well. The intimate nature of sex does not mix well with casual relationships. We cannot give ourselves away to just anyone, any place, any time, without an emotional armor to protect us. We can be hurt by partners who are still strangers in whom we have not invested enough to create a climate of trust, and from whom we expect nothing more than the immediate pleasure of the moment, the week, the month. Ironically, an irresponsible sexual encounter produces the same psychological effects as does a forbidding abstinence. Both promiscuity and sexual inhibition cause the suppression of emotions, the refusal of true intimacy, the loss of self. For those who value intimate relationship, with sex as one of the fulfilling expressions of it, commitment is necessary so that one can feel safe enough to remove the armor and live unencumbered.

Two questions arise: Can one be intimately committed to more than one person at a time? Can a commitment exist apart from marriage? In terms of society's interest in stable life, a man can responsibly be committed to more than one woman. He can provide for and sire children with more than one woman at the same time. Half the population in our culture is engaged in serial polygamy—several marriages over the course of a lifetime with one partner at a time and numerous children related to one another by stepparents and half parents. The rise in the divorce rate represents a shift in the definition of commitment. No longer is marriage circumscribed by economic necessity and the care of many children, as it was a generation ago, when the youngest child may have been reaching adulthood as parents died in their sixties. Life that is tied neither to the fertility of the land nor to the womb has radically changed human possibilities and has fostered affective individualism.

The expectations of individualism have connected romantic love to marriage. Economic life (work) is located outside the home, which has now become a "haven in a heartless world" and the provider of warmth and love. Since marriages are less and less bonded from economic necessity (especially for men), a failure to meet intimacy needs has become the impetus for divorce. If it were possible to be intimately committed to more than one person at a time, the divorce rate would surely not be so high. There are those who would disagree, and there are certainly exceptions to every thesis, but history and literature give witness over and over to the impossibility of multiple, simultaneous commitments of any depth. Experimental communes, like the nineteenth-century's Oneida Community, where multiple sex partners were permitted, invariably fail. Love affairs that run in tandem with marriages rarely remain synchronized. If some are successful at multiple commitments, they surely have decreased energy for other tasks, since involved relationships are very time-consuming.

If it is likely that human beings are capable of only one intimate commitment at a time, must it be in the context of marriage? The advantage of marriage over a voluntary private arrangement is its public nature. Long-term relationships do not rest on capricious feelings. They are sustained by an act of will. The promise to love and be faithful is a willful promise. The difficulty of keeping the promise is great, and the community's strength is needed in times of trouble. Just as the man and the woman make promises to each other in the marriage ceremony, so does the community promise to help them uphold their vows.

Where the community does not recognize a relationship as committed, the community has no mandate, indeed no authority, to help and support. Perhaps it is this lack that has led young people to be less inclined to make quick decisions about living together, as they were doing in the seventies. Once households are joined, all the irritations of conflicting habits and tastes pull at the seams of an agreement that was never carefully stitched and that has little outside support. Moving out is a lot more painful than moving in.

If society is upset and concerned about couples who break their marriage vows, it bears some responsibility. That is especially true of the church where the congregation has failed to keep its vows to support and nurture the marriage. In recent years we have, in many cases, erred on the side of permissiveness and "understanding." We have become increasingly casual about divorce. We have not wanted to be involved—not wanted to intrude on another's privacy. But marriage is not private, and every dissolution unravels the garment of our common life no less now than in centuries past. In our contemporary isolation we delude ourselves that it is not so.

But is it also possible for society to support and nurture committed relationships that exist outside of marriage? More and more people are answering yes to that question. Our tolerance for deviation from the norm increases as life becomes more complex and as we become more aware and more compassionate in response to that complexity.

There are older men and women, often widows and widowers, who wish to marry but do not want to change their legal status. Pension and Social Security benefits diminish with a new marriage. Anxious children fear they will no longer have claim to their dead parent's estate if the surviving parent remarries. There is prejudice against sex beyond the age of procreation. To marry would curtail income and disturb family relationships. There are also divorced women and a smattering of men who, in order to preserve alimony payments, do not remarry. There is less sympathy for such people, and yet it is only the present generation of younger women who realize that they cannot depend on marriage for economic security. Older women, who never imagined themselves divorced and thought they were economically contributing through homemaking, do need some kind of pension called alimony. The courts tend to award younger women who are unprepared to earn their living an allowance for a set period of time during which they are expected to prepare for economic independence.

Some couples live together in a kind of trial marriage before making a public commitment. In recent years more and more couples have listed the same addresses on their marriage licenses. Prohibitions against premarital sex have never been universal, nor are they explicitly biblical, nor have they been well kept once a couple is ready to explore the possibility of marriage. There is increasing experimentation with a trial period and increasing acceptance of it by the community. It is too soon to know if such openness leads to marriages that can withstand the onslaught of time. Decades ago anthropologist Margaret Mead recommended two-stage marriages in which final vows would not be taken until the couple had tested the relationship or was ready to have children. Nuns and monks have never been expected to commit their entire lives without a prior progression of professing vows over a period of years. We really cannot expect young people to keep lifelong vows (meaning fifty to seventy-five years) based on sketchy experience of one another.

Consideration of relationships outside of marriage leads us to consider homosexual unions. Some committed homosexual couples belie the popular reputation of the gay community as promiscuous. As long as we indiscriminately judge homosexual relationships as immoral, we unwittingly contribute to the inclination to promiscuity by not affirming commited relationships. From time to time gay couples have found church homes and have asked the pastor to bless and the congregation to accept their unions. But giving that blessing or offering that acceptance means running the risk of censure from the majority of both ordained and lay church persons. Official bodies of the church have not yet affirmed homosexuality as a public and morally acceptable lifestyle. Yet the American Psychiatric Association has removed homosexuality from its official category of mental illnesses, and gay people are less hidden among us. Inevitably it will become harder to exclude this group from the protection of the law and the affection of our hearts. Gay people are our sons and daughters, our brothers and sisters, our neighbors, our clergy, our physicians, our plumbers, our friends. We cannot uphold committed intimate relationships and the goodness of sexuality, and at the same time discriminate and moralize about homosexuality—a condition of life about which we know practically nothing except that it is.

Fortunately, there are a few compassionate and welcoming congregations all over this land who uphold and nurture committed gay couples. For now, that support is largely given in secret, but as practice precedes law, the time will come when the church will be more public and more honest in its recognition of these loving couples. That time will come unless we learn something about homosexuality that would place it in a category of life-destroying habit and choice. This last seems unlikely.

While the committed intimate relationship is the ideal context for sexuality, are there any alternatives to this ideal in which people can live their lives by self-conscious choice without falling under the judgment of the confessional?

Negativity against sexual activity is communicated to young children who show pleasure in touching themselves. Deep fears of masturbation have caused parents to reprove and threaten children with the supposed evils of self-stimulation. In the past these alleged evils included permanent brain damage and hair growth on the palms of the hands, not to mention eternal damnation. It is difficult for reason to penetrate early childhood training; fears instilled at an early age are difficult to erase.

It needs to be clear that present medical science unequivocally regards masturbation as neither morally evil nor biologically damaging, although that information is not yet entirely accepted by the population at large. Masturbation is a natural part of discovering bodily functions. The harm of masturbation is directly related only to the fear and negativity with which it has been regarded. People who are insensitive to and ignorant of their own sexual responses to varying kinds of stimulation are less able to adjust sexually to a partner. People who do not know their own erogenous sensations and who cannot speak of them will confuse and frustrate their partners.

Masturbation is not just a substitute for intercourse but an activity that may be engaged in for its own sake. It becomes problematic only when it is used as a defense against developing an intimate relationship with another. Sexual activity is at base not a solitary act but a sharing of life, one that is a wonderful human experience of community.

This century has also seen a changed attitude toward marriage as an expected vocation. No longer is it shameful to be unmarried. The word "spinster" has been relegated to archaic vocabulary. Unmarried women do not have to wear labels of derision as their maiden aunts did. Such proper maiden ladies of the past were cast into lifelong celibacy to be endured, frequently by becoming the paradigms of rigid virtue with ramrod backbones and judgmental airs. This is the moralistic spinster of the Wizard of Oz who persecutes Dorothy and her dog, Toto, first in Kansas and then as the Wicked Witch of the West in the magical land of Oz. These women as characterized in literature and community were both vicious gossips and fierce, self-appointed guardians of the community's righteousness. In a world that required daughters to become wives, they were stunted. They convinced themselves of the rightness of their moral stances, and society enforced their role by applauding it publicly.

One wonders about the inner sadness that many of these women have borne. No such burden was laid on the single male, for it was the normative practice for him to find sexual outlet among "loose" women of the society. There has been less acceptance recently as unmarried males have had to tolerate suspicions of homosexuality. In previous generations, the divorced person was almost nonexistent, so scandalous was divorce. The widowed person was the only remaining category of single adult. But with our present family upheavals, increased life expectancy, and the freedom not to marry, single adults comprise a larger and larger percentage of the population.

If a single adult does not want to live the celibate life and is not willing to be married, or is simply not emotionally ready for or capable of marriage, what are the alternatives that could still be called moral? Do we want to be in the position of saying that the satisfaction of sexual desire is an adequate basis for marriage? Do we have any alternatives other than the denial of sexual energy or the repression of sexual desire? Must we as Christians offer only an unachievable ideal or a word of judgment? Is not the gospel more loving than that?

Today few people in psychological or medical circles would suggest that a spouse's death, for example, means that the survivor must cap his or her sexuality forever. Sexual needs do not die with the death of one's partner. Yet when sex was inextricably tied to procreation, voluntary celibacy was the only alternative that society permitted. Clearly that may not be either the best or the only alternative today. If fullness of life is the goal of the Christian gospel, sexual abstinence may not always serve the goal. Are sexual relations between consenting single adults sometimes good? Are some sexual relationships beautiful, life-giving, beneficial, even though they are not lived out inside the marital bond? Surely the answer to these queries is yes. But what needs to be included in such relationships for them to be loving?

Sex between unmarried adults might be positive if it is a union of love and caring, not just a union of convenience and desire; if sex is shared only after other things have been shared, such as time, values, friendship, communication and a sense of deep trust and emotional responsibility, and if discretion is observed so that the relationship does not offend community values.

If the only sexual options for the single adult are a self-imposed abstinence that cannot be managed without physical distress and impairment of personality, or a committed but short-of-marriage relationship, then it could be said that an affair might be for some people the best choice, the most life-giving alternative. Under some circumstances, sexual intercourse outside marriage, or even outside the intent to marry, could be good and wise.

There is one final gray area. Are there any circumstances when sexual activity outside of marriage could be positive even while the marriage itself is still in force? The primacy and power of marriage need to be affirmed. It is a holy estate whose public vows pledge the partners to fidelity in sickness and in health, for richer or poorer, until parted by death. The sanctity of this relationship that enables the complete giving of a man and a woman to each other is what creates the proper context for complete sexual intimacy. When that relationship approaches the ideal, it touches the edges of holiness and has something of the nature of a sacrament about it. In the marital union, life can be shared in a way that it is shared nowhere else. All of live's beauty and wonder can be seen best when marriage fulfills its potential. But saluting the ideal does not create the ideal, and marital success is a constant dream but a rare accomplishment.

Nevertheless, the deliberate choice to compromise one's marriage by entering an extramarital relationship cannot be justified unless there are unusual, perhaps extreme, extenuating circumstances. If a marriage dies sexually, then before one partner or the other can justify an affair, that partner seems bound by the marriage vow to seek outside help and to address the disease in that sick marriage. If partners are not willing to do this, are they not finally guilty of breaking their word, damaging their character and their fidelity in seeking a sexual union outside of marriage? No support for such behavior can be found in the Christian gospel or in what are called the ethics of life, which grow out of that gospel.

If a wife loses interest in sex or if a husband becomes impotent, the marriage is crying out for help. Such sexual dysfunction does not confer a license for an affair. Yet, once that has been said, it must be stated that there are rare circumstances where one partner in a marriage is rendered sexually incompetent by physical disease, by accident, or by mental illness, and this forces the remaining partner to choose either a lifetime of sexual abstinence or the violation of the marriage vows. If the remaining partner can manage abstinence and maintain a satisfying life, that may be the best course. But if he or she cannot, are there options? There is the sheer physical release of masturbation, but that is a temporary, substitute solution at best. Lonely men have sought sexual outlets with prostitutes. But that is surely both an immoral and an illegal choice.

Another option could be an occasional sexual liaison with a series of acquaintances. It does not finally fill the empty places, for sex cries out for a primary relationship that is special and loving. Shallow sexual contact with a variety of partners cannot help but result in questions of identity and of the meaning of love itself.

The last alternative could be an affair with one who is loved, with whom many things are shared. This last alternative might be the best of the available options. But we cannot take the particular solution to the pain of broken humanity and raise it to the level of principle. The context of this conclusion is a compromised set of life circumstances where neither divorce nor counseling is a workable option. Many troubled people find healing, loving alternatives that are clearly short of the ideal but also short of the immoral.

Life conspires to move us all out of a moralistic legalism into more loving and compassionate attempts to discover the best alternatives for both the individual and the community in a broken, imperfect world. It is our conviction that Christianity itself compels us to reject any rigid system that applies rules indiscriminately to human beings. No one would distribute shoes to people without first checking for size. Surely that moral code whose purpose it is to support and improve life can not be dispensed without a similar check of size and fit.

Christianity can be separated from the repressive legalism of yesterday, a legalism that is neither biblical nor essential in the realities of the twentieth century. Christianity, however, does have standards and norms that need to be heard in the midst of the hedonistic revolution today. These principles are not so crisp or clear as the old prohibitions, but they are more loving and do spring from the sacredness of human life.

"You shall not commit adultery." This ancient commandment invites us to look at the depth of personhood, the depth of relationships, the sacredness of bodies, the fact that sex is powerful, and then decide how love, life, and being can be expressed so as to glorify the Creator in the sexual acts of the creature. Christians of the twentieth century are called to bear witness in word and deed in the arena of human sexuality.

Chapter 11

MICRO-THEFT AND MACRO-THEFT

"If our goods are not available to the community, they are stolen goods."
                                                              —MARTIN LUTHER

A small eastern North Carolina town in the early sixties claimed as one of its citizens a lovely black woman named Eva. Married, with two children, she lived in the clearly segregated part of that community. She was a high-school graduate but, as was true of most black people in that era in the South, few job opportunities were available other than domestic service. So she applied for a job in a home of one of her community's leading citizens and was hired. She worked from 8:00 a.m. to 5:00 p.m. each day. She tended the children, cooked, cleaned, washed, ironed, polished, and waxed. She had only one day off each week. Her starting salary was $15 a week. After she had worked in this home for three years her salary was increased to $18 a week. Her employer was a paragon of propriety, moral and upright. It never would have occurred to him or his socially prominent wife to rob a bank. Yet, with no qualms of conscience and in the name of "the going rate," they were quite willing to steal the labor of a powerless woman and to rob her children of an adequate diet, to say nothing of their human dignity. Never in their wildest imaginations would they have conceived of themselves as guilty of breaking the eighth commandment. Yet guilty they were.

The subleties of modern interpretation might relate this stealing of personhood to the original intent of the commandment, which was kidnapping, the literal stealing of a person. It was a common practice in the ancient world, where children were often stolen and sold into slavery. The Hebrew people, so recently escaped from Egypt, knew how slavery devastated life, they never allowed the memory of the Egyptian captivity to die. Consequently, the impulse to kidnap diminished, and this commandment came to refer primarily to property and possessions and the right of private ownership.

In its most concrete form, "You shall not steal" means you shall not take what is not your own. In a wider perspective, however, this commandment raises searching questions about how society defines ownership and about the individual's right to ownership. Where, for example, does the responsibility for the common good of social structures reside? Does it rest with the individual, or with social structures? What is the meaning of private property? What are its limits? When is an owner a steward and when an exploiter? To whom do natural resources belong? Can they be used by those who hold title with no regard for preserving them or for the concerns of future generations? When does a concern for profit collide with the common good? At what point does legislation governing the environment, equitable tax structures, comprehensive health care, or world trade become the necessary social response to the injunction "You shall not steal?"

Dr. Joseph Fletcher, in his book *Moral Responsibility,* distinguishes between what he calls "microethics," personal ethics seen in microcosm, and "macroethics," corporate ethics seen in macrocosm. Microethics refer to acts of an individual, one's particular choices in human relationships. Macroethics refer to acts of the whole society that affect that whole society, and perhaps other societies as well. The two are certainly interrelated. When macroethics are designed to promote universal justice, corporate activity redresses grievances and creates a climate of unity in a socially responsive world. This activity has the dual effect of curtailing systemic evil and minimizing the individual's impulse to act in antisocial ways. A world in which all injustice is overcome is named the kingdom of God. Until that kingdom comes, human need will elicit response from both the private or individual and the corporate, or public, sectors. Two factors, the recognition of our imperfect order and our human response to the suffering that accompanies life in such a world, bring all actions to ethical scrutiny. Both microethics and macroethics are important to our explorations of the eighth commandment, "You shall not steal."

When we examine life on the microethical level, we discover that our possessions imitate our personalities. Teilhard de Chardin believed that the products of our genius, the work of hands, heart, and

intellect, are extensions of ourselves. Such self-generated possessions are the result of the human impulse to create, to act in the world
the way God acts, by creating as a primary manifestation of being.
The modern era has altered methods of production and the products.
In the process, perhaps our being has been altered as well.

Before industrialization, people lived and labored at home. Home
as the locus of work, the place where cottage industry and farming
produced the necessities and many of the luxuries of life, gave way
first to manufacturing and industrial plants and later to offices. Today,
a substantial majority of workers produce information and services
rather than goods. Material possessions are accumulated by purchase
rather than by craft. Though most of us no longer touch the soil that
grows our food or weave the cloth that covers our bodies, our
possessions—bought or made—continue to reveal our personalities
and characters. We choose our possessions in response to our perceived needs as human beings.

The late psychologist Abraham Maslow listed those human needs
in an order that ascends from those required for basic survival—food,
shelter, clothing, physical safety—to a higher order that attends to
self-development—belonging, love, recognition, and "self-actualiz-
ation," what we might call fullness of being. The phenomenon we
call materialism is a function of human personality stuck at the level
of providing for basic survival needs in a repetitive, redundant orgy of
acquisition. The cycle of a lifetime spent accumulating multiple
houses, vehicles, and clothes is a spiritual problem, a refusal to
become ourselves.

The ascetic emphasis in the Judeo-Christian tradition has the
reputation of being anti-material and anti-creation. Extremists who
engaged in severe denials and mortifications of the flesh, in which
self-inflicted bodily injuries were a regular part of the spiritual
discipline, were certainly anticreationists and spiritual perverts. But
the major thrust of ascetic discipline was training directed toward
satisfying universally acknowledged human needs with the least
amount of time, energy, and wealth possible. The ascetics realized
that significant accumulation of private property is life-consuming. If
we wish to achieve a high level of development and to work creatively,
it is imperative that we not bind ourselves to acquiring and taking care

of too many things. Materialism is not a sin because things are intrinsically evil. It is a sin because our attachment to and investment in our possessions prevent us from looking beyond them.

The spiritually authentic responses to the physical world and to ownership of material possessions were traditions of simplicity rather than traditions of denial. A life of simplicity is not anti-material. It is a recognition that significant accumulations of private property are demanding of time and attention, both of which are precious commodities.

Materialism aside, ownership of property is a part of society's organization. The well-meaning eighteenth-century Hasidic teacher Rebbe Wolfe of Zbaraj, who disclaimed all personal ownership so that any thief who stole from him could not be judged guilty of breaking the eighth commandment, was more naive then generous. Given the necessity of private ownership, our sense of self-interest demands that there be a general respect for property, that there be a strongly accepted public attitude of considerate regard for ownership, public and private. Otherwise chaos and anarchy reign, and the necessity to protect what is our own keeps us perpetually on guard.

When a society's assumptions about rights to ownership begin to be challenged, public faith is shaken, trust diminishes, the crime rates soar, burglar-alarm systems proliferate, and a vigilante mentality abrogates the public responsibility to maintain law and order. Offensive tactics against threat aggravate the already-hostile environment and magnify the danger. When those symptoms appear, when neighbor has become the potential enemy, then that society is in a state of seige. Increased police protection and political oratory about law and order are symptoms of a population that exists at a survival level. As symptoms, and not cures, repressive measures reinforce distrust and exacerbate fear. Police protection and campaign rhetoric touch the surface but not the core of the problem. What these symptoms disclose is the breakdown of the cultural values that glue society together. When there is neither an accepted norm for what is right and what is wrong, nor a shared assumption about the acquiring and ownership of private property, then social disintegration follows. Unless the values of a society can be restated or revised and then enforced by both the law and the will of the people, that society will not endure.

No society can flourish or even survive unless there are commonly held political, social, and economic values. These values are concerned with the process of transferring and sharing power, and the acceptable methods for maintaining and improving the quality of life. When crime proliferates, it does so for three reasons. First, in times of social unrest, deliberate illegal acts are done in order to draw attention to unjust law. These acts are legally defined as crimes but fall into the realm of civil disobedience. Secondly, new laws make certain acts illegal that formerly were legal. Environmental-protection laws and the banking and security laws that hold corporations and their executives accountable to the public trust are examples of legislation that represents major changes in the philosophy of law. A third reason for acceleration of crime is economic, social, and political deprivation. When large numbers of alienated groups or individuals are prevented from achieving a quality of life that the culture affirms and promotes, then the whole of society will be reduced to choosing between living in a police state or living in anarchy. That is a dreadful choice. However, in urban American today, that is increasingly the choice before us. Unless we are willing and able to redress injustice and transform the breeding grounds of crime, this nation will undoubtedly choose a police state, or even unofficially accept the protection of the Mafia and other self-appointed control groups, for the human inclination is to choose safety over freedom. When life is precarious, freedom is a luxury but security an essential. The best of all possible worlds is a peaceful freedom, but that cannot be achieved unless the society is based on radical justice that affirms the worth of every life. Only in such a society would those who disregard the just order and violate the society's rules be few enough in number that minimum police protection would adequately guarantee the public safety.

When a society agrees on its norms for collective living, rules are articulated and penalties for infractions are devised. The result is a code of law. In a democracy, that code can always be changed by the elected representatives who respond to the will of the people. (However, democracy tends toward a tyranny of the majority, so constitutional safeguards that protect minorities from exploitation are essential.) Law is constantly reinterpreted in the light of contemporary circumstances. Therefore the law has a certain flexibility in a living society.

Every code of every people, however, whether that code be ancient or modern, Western or Eastern, capitalist, communist, or socialist, prohibits taking by force or stealth what is not one's own, what one has not earned, and what one has no right to claim. Stealing comes in many forms and by many names: burglary, larceny, embezzling, hijacking, shoplifting, plagiarizing, gypping, looting, swindling, cheating, deceiving, concealing defects, falsely labeling, giving short measures, exaggerating quality. Stealing comes also in the dishonest claims of false advertisement, in not paying an honest wage, in not doing an honest day's work.

The ways we steal from one another seem limited only by the imagination. Some take advantage of ignorance or manipulate the bereaved to make expensive purchases. Others steal by doing shoddy work, raising prices for windfall profit during shortages, coercing children to lie about their age to get a cheaper rate, falsifying entries on income-tax forms, and sending phone messages long distance without paying. So pervasive is this game we play against the system that we hardly think of it as crime.

The eighth commandment called Israel, and later called the Christian community, to a life of radical individual and corporate honesty in obedience to the God who established our covenant.

Nothing in the balance of this chapter should in any way minimize the importance of this microethical level of behavior to which this commandment spoke in the past, and still speaks today. We must, however, go further into historic and present attitudes toward property, both public and private, in order to explore the commandment "You shall not steal" in a macroethical setting.

The biblical doctrine of creation, which proclaims the holiness and the goodness of the material world, questions the improper use of material things, but not their moral value. The Bible is not ambiguous about economic issues. In spite of a tendency to equate prosperity with God's favor, the Bible constantly enjoins us not to accumulate wealth or to exploit the poor. Our contemporary economic values are clearly challenged.

Leviticus 25 called for a jubilee celebration once every fifty years, in which loans expired, indentured servants were freed, and each family returned to the ancestral property. Though there is no evidence that this jubilee law was ever followed, its intent was to make a theological statement about ownership and about our relationship with God. The land was a gift of God, even as an inheritance to God's people. It could never be considered private property to be sold at will or leased indefinitely. Had this law been observed, it would have resulted in a redistribution of wealth every fifty years, for wealth like everything else, belongs to God.

The Bible does not distinguish between the haves and the have-nots nearly so much as between the have-too-muches and the have-not-enoughs. The gospels recognize that any material possessions can be dangerous: "No one can serve two masters"; "it is easier for a camel to go through the eye of a needle than for a rich man to enter the Kingdom of God"; "where your treasure is, there will your heart be also"; "do not lay up for yourselves treasures on earth." Wealth can corrupt, and when it does, it begets greed, lust, and exploitation. Sometimes wealth encourages people to become benefactors and philanthropists, but unfortunately the generosity of the wealthy is mostly directed to relieving the symptoms of the social malaise rather than to addressing the root causes of injustice.

If it is difficult to be rich and virtuous, it is equally difficult to be poor and virtuous. Poverty almost always diminishes its victims, producing bitterness and despair. The poor, frustrated and fearful, harm themselves or others. Such persons kill psychic pain with anesthetizing drugs, erupt violently, or escape into insanity. Let us not suppose that the poor are any less caught by materialism than the rich. Our consumer society affects all levels of the population. The dreams of the poor can match in material content the tangible wealth that the rich possess. The use and distribution of property and wealth, in both scarcity and abundance, is an issue for all of us regardless of our socio-economic position.

The right use of our wealth is a primary way to act out Jesus' summary of the law: to love God with our whole heart, soul, and mind, and to love our neighbor as ourself. To believe that "the earth is the Lord's and the fullness thereof" (Psalm 24) and that all are charged to be temporary stewards of God's world frees us to set aside self-serving and shortsighted economic tactics and to develop new ways of relating to one another and to the world we live in. The prevailing myth that we are conquerors and subduers of the earth by divine mandate continually needs to be challenged.

Changing behavior changes hearts. We might begin with changing our language, since words are carriers of the cultural myths that inform habits and customs. The Book of Common Prayer claims that human beings are the "rulers of creation." Because we persist in our arrogant belief that being rulers means having the right, nay the duty, to operate in this world as if it were created for our benefit and pleasure alone, we might substitute "stewards" for "rulers." We need words that indicate an awareness of our dependence on one another and on our environment. We belong to the earth every bit as much as the earth belongs to us. We need to think of our work of developing civilization in terms of shepherding, midwifery, husbandry, tending the sacred treasures that are all around us.

In our increasingly crowded and despoiled world, it becomes more and more obvious that we do not have the right to continue in the unchecked accumulation of wealth and unlimited use of resources that has been our pattern of life, woven into our thinking as the Western way of progress. Our pioneer ancestors never imagined where their industrious initiative would lead. Settlers in the old West, where one's closest neighbor was miles away, did not have to be sensitive to the infringements on personal life space that are daily abrasives in congested housing complexes and on highway cloverleafs. Our pioneer ancestors set self-sufficiency as a virtue and an attainable good. Today we cannot escape our mutual dependency. We know now that we share a common environment. There will be no future generations if we continue to pollute our rivers, lakes, and seas and to rob the land of its minerals and its capacity to sustain life. Profit can no longer be the solitary goal of any commercial enterprise, large or small. Business must be socially attuned to the price that society will have to pay now and later for the extravagant profits that permit us to overfeed and pamper ourselves. This is of particular moment to Americans who make up six percent of the world's population yet consume thirty-five percent of its resources. Can a world long survive divided between those who diet and those who starve?

Other questions also arise. Economic questions are invariably interwoven around and into the body politic, whose larger questions are of international proportions. Do the natural resources of the earth belong to the God who created them to be used by all for mutual benefit? Or do they belong to those who happen to own the land that contains them? Or do they belong to those who have the technology to mine, dredge, and retrieve? If we allow the earth's resources to be held captive by rights of property ownership, then more questions come to the fore. What are the obligations of an owner or developer to the society as a whole? Should limits be placed on individual profits drawn from the riches of the earth? Should the stockholders of oil companies be the primary beneficiaries of the offshore oil that lies, theoretically, under international seas? What economic theories and ethical precepts make it possible for an individual such as the late Howard Hughes to accumulate nearly two billion dollars during the same period in which the unemployment rate of the nation soared to nearly ten percent, and massive starvation occurred in the sub-Sahara regions of Africa. For all our sakes, an appropriate balance must be struck between private acquisition of wealth and public needs.

No economic system is just and fair to all in every circumstance. Until such a system is devised, support of the free-enterprise system and its necessary corollary of private property may be the best of few alternatives. No matter how a society organizes itself, it is the desire to become an owner and to share in the symbols of success that feeds human motivation. Any system that incorporates a work ethic must have incentives built into it. We are inspired to work by the hope of adequate recompense for labor, and rewards for industry and ingenuity. A complete state socialism practices just distributions of wealth and resources but fails to maintain the productivity and enthusiasm that accompany competitive creativity. At the same time, an unbridled laissez-faire capitalist system is as destructive to human freedom as any communist system might be, for unrestrained capitalism will concentrate wealth and power among the few and eventually eliminate competition by monopolizing the means of production and exploiting the labor of the majority. Karl Marx accurately predicted these conditions as precursors to revolution, but he did not grasp the ability of the capitalistic system to temper its excesses with social legislation and thus to secure the good life for large numbers of people by providing for continuing, peaceful revolutions and power distributions.

Socially restrained free enterprise can be appreciated in a way unregulated capitalism can not. The best friends of American capitalism are those things against which conservatives rail: antitrust laws, graduated income taxes, inheritance taxes, Social Security, Medicare and Medicaid programs, and all the other legislation that has modified the capitalist system and distributed wealth, provided adequate public services, and developed, in the process, the great middle class that makes the American economy strong. That same middle class, however, errs when it assumes that democracy ensures equal opportunity and the freedom to take advantage of it. There is a middle-class bias toward the underclasses that falsely assumes character defect as the cause for failure to participate in the American dream of prosperity and happiness.

The American Constitution and the Bible share the anthropological insight that our self-centered, sinful nature causes us to operate from the vantage point of self-interest. For this reason our founders determined that no one person or one branch of government should ever be allowed to achieve total power. Our human tendencies to fulfill our own wishes at the expense of others and without moral discrimination inclines us to misuse power, and power corrupts in proportion to its degree of autonomy. Government is effective, says our Constitution, when there is a system of checks and balances that coordinates the independent functions of our executive, legislative, and judicial branches. Those safeguards realisticially acknowledge two truths: government's need for the power to make public decisions that can be implemented, and the potential for distortion in decision making that accompanies group and individual self-interest.

The authors of the Constitution did not quite so well understand powerlessness or guard against its effects. Because of the self-centeredness of human nature, powerless people will be exploited. When workers had no power, there were sweatshops, starvation wages, long hours, and abusive child-labor practices. Even John Locke, an enlightened political philosopher for his day, and a champion of laissez-faire capitalism, wrote: "The children of the poor must be required to work in the industrial enterprise beginning at age three."

Unchallenged power carries with it the seeds of nonpeaceful revolution. Human beings will not tolerate exploitation indefinitely, for it militates against the sacred image of God that is within each of us. Labor unions, for example, that confront owners with collective power are an essential ingredient in a healthy capitalist/socialist society, for there can be no real justice unless power is shared.

Exploitation and victimization are nothing less than forms of stealing: the stealing of a person's time, effort, and hope. This is a social violation of the eighth commandment on the macroethical scale.

Enlightened Christians work to remove every vestige of exploitation from society. In obedience to this commandment against stealing, Christians will oppose racism at every level and in every form, they will support the rights of labor to organize for collective bargaining, and they will work for the passage of legislation against the sexist exploitation of women. Christianity is a worldly religion of incarnation, not a spiritual religion of ethereal concerns.

Those Christians who are stockholders, while appreciating the benefits of the American system, have a duty to speak out against the unethical practices of companies that exploit the natural resources of small and powerless countries by undergirding the economies of oppressive, totalitarian regimes. In those marginal countries, factories abuse poor workers by allowing unsafe conditions and paying slave wages. Land whose products support the various consumer appetites of Americans has become unavailable to grow food for third-world citizens. For instance, a field in Nigeria that once raised grain for a starving native population was turned to the production of gladioli for the American market.

Such activities sow a deep enmity that someone someday will have to reap. Christians and other responsible citizens who abhor the devaluing of life need to demonstrate humane and just behavior in their own lives, including their consumer practices. They must become involved, then, in political processes that can effect change in the whole economic structure, domestic and foreign. The first step is a willingness to see and to admit the present level of duplicity.

The test of a just society has always been the manner in which it treats its weakest and least productive members. Good intentions never protect the old, young, sick, or mentally and physically handicapped among us. To assume so is to adopt a stance of naive optimism. Only willful, determined action will protect those who cannot protect themselves. A utopian society is organized so that no one is disenfranchised and no one, therefore, is a victim. That ideal can be approached by a sharing of power that will minimize life-destroying exploitation. Power will have to flow away from the powerful and toward the powerless. That dynamic flow of power is the essence of revolution. The powerful will of course consider such a flow destabilizing. From their short-range perspective, it always is.

An equitable sharing of power will require an appropriate portion of private wealth to support the needs of the whole society. A just society will levy adequate and fair taxes to support excellent public school systems, public parks, libraries, educational and health facilities. Taxes are needed to provide also for the development of culture—art, music, dance, drama—to enrich public life. Society determines the balance between private and public enterprises, but it is in the deepest vested interest of those who possess the lion's share of this world's goods to be the most concerned about the public welfare. Some have. The Roosevelts and the Rockefellers are families of great wealth who have contributed leaders with social consciences to our national life.

Private altruism is, however, an insufficient response. The social conscience must respond as well. What does it say about the soul of a nation when, in an economic downturn, the leaders of that nation attempt to balance the federal budget by cutting social programs that feed, shelter, educate, and generally assist the poor and the weak, while at the same time continuing to maintain a defense establishment dedicated to war games that pretend we can secure our future with the unlimited escalation of weapons and power tools that are designed to victimize? Of course the ultimate question of stewardship is whether we will turn the Lord's earth and its inhabitants to nuclear ash—stealing the future in one misguided moment.

If we manage to avoid self-annihilation, the institutional church needs to turn its attention toward the challenging task of helping this society reconceive and revalue its system of priorities. In this period of opulent materialism, an increasing disparity is developing between material values and moral values, between private wealth and public need. Christian teaching compels us to rise above our self-interest and to affirm the values that establish the common good. Twentieth-century people understand interdependence in a way that escaped notice in the past. We do not slip into the kingdom of God one by one; we go together or not at all. There is no true or lasting private gain at the cost of social impoverishment. Private gain as the primary goal of life presumes that individuals can create a world of their liking apart from the destinies of others. Similarly, those who direct their lives toward an end of their own salvation live in the heretical conceit of believing that God plays favorites, is willing to give up on "lost sheep," or is more interested in the endangered human species than the endangered timber rattlesnake. Individualistic piety bets on future heavenly existence against life as it is, and in the process devalues God's own handiwork. If we really have faith in an eternal destiny ruled by the God made known in history, we will work all the harder to make "this island home" a place where God can live among us, and we will give up our escapist irresponsible dreams of apocalyptic rapture.

God incarnate in human history activates the mandates of the eighth commandment, raised to the macrocosmic level. Living in justice in this world as a good steward of God's bounty, maintaining individual, personal life and yet caring for every legitimate public need, removing every vestige of expoitation, protecting the environment for today's and tomorrow's generations, and being honest in every individual transaction—all of these extend the spirit of the commandment in, through, and around the whole of our complicated and complex lives. "You shall not steal." The echoes of this law reverberate into every nook and cranny of our existence, and there is nowhere to hide. Those simplistic people who continue to parrot statements such as "The church should stick to the Bible and not get involved with politics" misconstrue the unity of thought and behavior, because what we believe and how we act can never be separated on any level of life. It is through politics and economics as well as through individual morality that we are called to build a just society in which we love God with our hearts, our minds, our souls, and our strengths, and in which we love our neighbors as ourselves.

Chapter 12

THE HUMAN TONGUE

"The liar's punishment is not that he is not believed but that he
cannot believe anyone else."   —GEORGE BERNARD SHAW

An ancient Talmudic story tells of a king who sent out two
of his servants with very interesting instructions. One was asked to
bring back the greatest thing that humanity has ever known, and the
other was asked to bring back the worst and most destructive thing
that humanity has ever known. According to the story, both returned
with the human tongue.

Speech is the most precise way we communicate ourselves to
others. The refusal to speak in dialogue isolates and locks the self into
a prison of misunderstanding and loneliness. Conversely, a super-
fluity of words fills the conversational space and prevents exchange.
Our tongues reveal our true selves, even when we try to use words to
conceal. The tongue is the two-edged sword that can be used either to
hurt or to heal.

From the tongue come forth the words that build relationships,
express love, offer peace, pronounce blessings, inspire to action. It
was the tongue that gave Isaiah, Joan of Arc, Abraham Lincoln, and
Winston Churchill their immense power and their tremendous gifts of
leadership. Each of these people moved a nation merely with words.
They could articulate heartfelt desires and mobilize the resources of
their people. But from the same human tongue come also rumor, lies,
slander, and curses.

It is interesting to note that one-fifth of the decalogue concerns use
of the tongue: "You shall not take the name of the Lord your God in
vain" and "You shall not bear false witness." To misuse the divine
name reveals separation from God. To lie under oath reveals separation from both neighbor and from self. "Separation" and "alienation" are the words used by Martin Heidegger and other existential
thinkers to describe sin. Sin is the condition of apartness that slips to

lostness and then plunges into the deepest despair that disordered life can know. Destructive words grease the slide of decline.

The sins of the tongue can be premeditated, but they can also be deceptions or twisted truths that fool even the one who utters them.

Alice Roosevelt Longworth in her later years, when her mobility was limited, received her friends in a sitting room decorated with a cross-stitched denim cushion that announced, "If you haven't got anything good to say about anyone, come and sit by me." That story usually brings a smile not only to those who knew Princess Alice, as the daughter of Teddy Roosevelt was long called, but to all the rest of us who know about human beings and gossip. Most of us enjoy gossip—either the telling or the hearing, or both. When we think about gossip we think in negativities: "It is not nice to gossip." "Gossip is hurtful or harmful." But gossip comes in a variety of forms. Some of it is truly idle, indulgent talk, an innocent exchange of information about the lives of people we know—who is moving, who is pregnant, who has a new job, who is sick, and so on. Such gossip tends to remain innocuous as long as the gossiper knows firsthand that what is being said is true. As soon as we begin to pass on hearsay or to embellish the facts with interpretations and motivations that the gossiper has invented, trouble is not far behind.

Passing on gossip gives a certain satisfaction. It makes the gossipers feel important: he or she has secret sources of information, is "in the know." Gossip also serves to give the appearance, at least, of entering into the privacies of lives that are normally hidden from view. It is a vicarious experience of life that titillates without the risk of involvement or self-exposure. It is voyeurism. The more important the subject of the gossip, the more pleasurable the telling. The inclination to embellish, embroider, and massage the nub of truth that is buried in all gossip turns that gossip into rumor. Rumor is like the child's game of "telephone," where the leader whispers a message that is whispered down the line to each in turn. There is so much subjective mishearing that the last person to hear repeats a very different message from the original.

Rumors fly in a time of crisis. Wildly circulating rumors indicate that people are stirred up about something. Situations are either getting better or getting worse. Rumors accentuate and aggravate emotions. Rumor flies on the wings of curiosity, wish, fear, and hostility. Something in us wants to believe both the best and the worst in people. The epistle of James speaks about the potential evil of a lying tongue: "It is a pest," he writes, "full of deadly poison" (James 3).

What we say tells as much about us as persons as it does about the subjects of our gossip. We gossip only about things and people who capture our interest. As a rule, Westerners do not discuss the price of camels in Afghanistan or the peccadillos of African chieftains. We gossip about our own curiosities.

Human attributes and characteristics are sometimes personified in literature and art. Depictions of gossip and rumor are invariably portrayed as women, as in these lines from the *Aeneid*:

> "Rumor! What evil can surpass her speed?
> Foul, whispering lips, and ears, that catch it all . . . .
>   She can cling . . .
> To vile invention and malignancy wrong,
> Or mingle with her words some tiding true."

It was Shakespeare who firmly tied the image of woman to gossip. The original word "gossip" was "godsip." It meant "related through God," and was used as a title for a sponsor at baptism—a godparent. The word evolved into a word that meant "friend." Then Shakespeare commented that when two women friends get together, gossip is sure to follow.

The gender association is not really surprising, since gossip tends to stories about people, and women typically have a curiosity and high interest in relationships. Though it is difficult to preserve stereotyped generalizations anymore, it still appears that female conversations veer toward "people talk," while male conversations are weighted toward activities and ideas. Women are often the family members who are designated to write letters to parents, to children away from home, to people who used to be neighbors and have moved away. For those who are charged with keeping relationships intact, gossip is their stock in trade. Of course, men gossip too. We have only to remember how the machinery of government in our nation's capital is fueled by gossip and rumor.

When gossip is motivated by wish, fear, or hatred, as it often is, it carries condemnation, not compassion, intends evil, not good. Magnifying faults and undermining reputations are attempts to prove oneself righteous. The spreading of morbid stories gives relief to one's own fears and offers the illusion of having safely escaped tragedy oneself. Part of the appeal of gossiping is the feeling of superiority and security it allows us to feel. "At least I'm not like that" or "Thank God that terrible thing didn't happen to me." Well, we *could* be like that and it *could* happen to us. In our heart of hearts we recognize the truth behind malicious tongues. The more we know our inner natures, the more we can empathize with the victims of gossip and be compassionate and understanding.

Since human beings are inclined to gossip in one way or another, we need to find ways to avoid contributing to and being swept along with the tide of gossip and rumor that flows away from truth and becomes malevolent. The advice of the book of James was to keep busy visiting the widows and orphans who could not provide for themselves. When idleness is reduced, gossip will be reduced as well, he counsels.

Consultants who work with groups torn by conflict recommend that gossip and rumor be passed on complete with the name of the person who told it. That takes the anonymity away and locates responsibility for the consequences of hurtful rumors. The best way to deal with the impulse to gossip that has the potential to hurt is to be very well acquainted with our own fears, angers, wishes, hostilities, and hatreds. To come to some acceptance of our own fears and anxieties and to admit that we do not always feel love towards others removes the impulse to peek at others' vulnerability. We cannot elevate our self-esteem at the expense of others when we are truthful about our own less-than-lovely natures.

Gossip and rumor are related to truth as legend is related to history. Somewhere something happened that grew and took on an unfactual and fanciful story line in the repeated telling. Those who pass on the stories become less and less aware of their prevarications; they believe the truth of their tales. Lying is another matter. Lies are intentional untruths. The conscious mind knows the words to be false.

How are we served by bending or disregarding the truth? A lie is an attempt to restructure reality so that we can have it the way we want it. We lie to improve image, to build prestige, to overcome a sense of inadequacy. Lying is a protection against revelation when we fear that if others really knew what we are like, we would be despised and rejected. We lie when we fear the truth will be punishing. We lie to people whom we expect to be unforgiving and uncompromising. We lie as sycophants who flatter in the hope of gaining favor.

Lying as a defensive posture is common enough that authority persons in some occupations meet lies as often as truth. Police and Internal Revenue Service auditors have come to expect falsehood; they must be among the world's most cynical and disillusioned people. The police who control traffic hear so many false statements they are sometimes surprised by candid truth.

One Saturday afternoon in late December as I sped through a thirty-five-mile zone at fifty miles per hour, the red lights of an unmarked patrol car flashed in the rearview mirror. I pulled over, got out of my car, and went to meet the officer. I had just come from a wedding and was dressed in the black clerical garb of my profession. Sternly he asked, "What's your hurry, Reverend?"

"Do you want the truth, or a wild story?" I responded.

"The truth would be refreshing," he replied.

"The truth is I just finished conducting a wedding, and I have been angry all day that anyone would be so inconsiderate as to schedule a wedding on the one Saturday in December when the Washington Redskins are playing the Dallas Cowboys in a return match, with a shot at the Super Bowl going to the winner." I told him that I knew if I rushed home from that reception, I might get to see the last five minutes of that game. "That's why I'm speeding," I said.

There was a pause. "You know, Reverend," the policeman said smiling, "I think I understand that. That seems to ring true. I wouldn't want to hold you up any longer. Merry Christmas!"

And the truth will set you free!

The commandment forbidding false witness was initially set in a court of law. To give false testimony knowingly against someone on trial struck a blow at the very heart of the system of human justice. Perjury was severely punished. The biblical penalty for false witness was to give to the false witness the same penalty his or her lies tried to inflict upon a prospective victim. The Romans hurled the court liar to a certain death from a cliff. The Egyptians cut off noses and ears of public liars.

Our systems of justice cannot tolerate the destruction of reputation and life with a lie. Without trust there is no freedom. As Nietzsche said, "It is not that you lied to me but that I can no longer believe you—that is what has distressed me." Deception destroys sacred trust, which is essential to our living together.

The ruinous power of a lie is told in a familiar rabbinic tale. A character-assassinating falsehood based on circumstantial evidence was told of a much-respected elderly man. When the victim heard of it, he confronted his accuser, who apologized and asked if there were anything that he could do to right the terrible wrong that had been done. The elderly man walked into the bedroom and picked up a feather pillow from the bed. Taking out his knife, he split the pillow open, went to the second-floor window of this house and dumped the feathers from that pillow into the breeze. They blew in every direction.

"Yes," he said, "there is something you can do. You can go out now and gather up all of those feathers and put them back inside this pillow."

"But, sir," the other man protested, "that is impossible. I could never recover each of those tiny feathers."

"Yes, it is impossible," the old man agreed. "Just as impossible as it is for you to take back all the hurt and the pain your malicious rumor and absolute lie has done to me. You cannot recover the suspicion that you have sown, the damage to my character."

Conscience may accuse calculating and knowing liars. The discomfort and pain of healthy guilt encourages us to make amends and to avoid repetition. But a more insidious and pervasive dishonesty is the social lie that arises from being unaware that one's judgment is based on insufficient data. Testimony as opinion is subjective interpretation of facts and events that are filtered through the bias of limited experience. We are all confined by our subjective filters, but error comes when we confuse opinion with perfect truth and proclaim our partial and particular truths as the whole of reality. It is the mark of the bigot and the fanatic to elevate a piece of truth to absolute status and insist that all the rest of us must organize our lives as they do—in the name of their truth, their experience, their incomplete witness. The prejudice of bigots is by its very nature shortsighted. Fanatics cannot survive the distractions of multiple certainties. All of us "see in a mirror dimly," but some of us know it and some of us hold on to the delusion that what we understand fully.

In a national church council debate some years ago, a black churchman made some highly critical, disparaging statements about the United States of America. He called it an "oppressive state," a state that broke the spirit of many of its citizens, grinding them under in a quest for profit. He was immediately challenged by a white male executive vice president of a major United States corporation, who extolled America's virtues as if they were divine attributes. He praised American business as an altruistic system that would save the world economy. Faults were glossed over or dismissed as being inconsequential, since Americans, he claimed, were quick and efficient in their problem solving.

This was not a debate between truth and untruth, nor was it an argument that pitted fact against fact, though both speakers were convinced of the objectivity of their thoughts. Rather, here were two competing perceptions of reality, both of which were true—true to the life experiences of the respective speakers, neither of which necessarily matched the experiences of the audience.

The black American knew himself to be a citizen of a nation where the rights and expectations of full adult citizenship were curtailed because he was a person of color. He had grown up in poverty, part of a de facto class system. The right to vote was denied him until the later years of his life. He had been educated in an inferior, segregated school system that used the hand-me-down textbooks from the white schools, whose board members shamelessly touted the black school system as "separate but equal." This man had observed that blacks were the last to be hired in prosperous times and first to be fired in depressed times. He watched American leaders panic when white unemployment reached six percent, knowing that black unemployment never had sunk below ten percent or much under fifty percent for black males under twenty-five years of age and living in depressed urban areas. He knew that the epidemic of drug use, long a part of ghetto life, was never acknowledged until middle-class white teenagers got caught by the dreadful habit.

This black man listened to white politicians talk about the abuses of the welfare system. He had observed government leaders placing the priority of a balanced budget above human need while at the same time being quite willing to rescue a struggling aircraft corporation with massive federal aid. He had seen America open its heart to resettle thousands of Vietnamese refugees and to find jobs for them, while the native black unemployment remained at an all-time high.

The black citizenry watched these Vietnamese victims settle into homes in neighborhoods from which the black American population had been systematically excluded. Blacks watched minor concessions and token integration being made, while the power base of the society changed very little. They saw segregation being preserved even where it was no longer legal. While all this was happening, the gap between the average white income and the average black income continued to widen, giving the lie to statements about improvement in race relations.

The facts of life as this black church leader knew them informed his critical words about his country. From his vantage point his words were objective, for they were certainly real and true for him and his black brothers and sisters.

The white male executive vice president of the large corporation also spoke his own truth. He described his country as a land of unlimited opportunity, where a person with ability could climb the corporate ladder to success and affluence, for that was his experience. He observed that the ingenuity and ability of his peers was rewarded. He saw the affluent, prosperous middle class in this country being created by a free economy, and he saw abundant resources being directed to alleviate the distresses of humanity.

Having never been the victim of prejudice, he was critical of those who could not and did not make it within the system as he had. He probably believed that those who do not succeed really were inferior. He was confident that people like himself who ruled the business establishment did so because they had innate ability. He had no sense of how prejudice distorts perception. Without that perspective he turned on the man whose citizenship was of a different order and accused him, by implication, of being an ingrate, a charlatan, a revolutionary, and even a communist.

Both men were accurate in their descriptions of life as life had come to them, but both were guilty of ignorance. Each had taken a partial experience and projected it into a whole experience. They had then defined their partial views and subjectivities as objective truth. Unaware of what they were doing, both of them had borne false witness against their neighbor.

Like the six blind men who felt separate parts of an elephant's anatomy and then gave six different descriptions of what an elephant was like, we know only as much as we are willing and able to touch. Since we tend to gravitate to the familiar, many of us choose to live in ghettos of one kind or another where the people, scenery, problems, and aspirations are similar. Country-club cocktail parties are as predictable and self-defeating as the nightly street-corner gatherings of poor city folk. All such "ghetto" people—rich, poor, and in between—talk only to one another, think and act in a narrow swath of life, and spend their time reinforcing one another's prejudices.

To be unaware of the infinite possibilities and combinations of life that extend individual truth into a connecting larger truth means that the mirrors of our minds deceive us. Experience, even when misinterpreted and falsely applied to others, has such authority as a test of reality that, as Samuel Coleridge observed, most people are right in what they affirm and wrong in what they deny. The false witness of the unconscious mind takes shape in the words of those denials.

Partial truth as false witness is a particular and prevalent sin among those of us who call ourselves Christians. God can be experienced but not explained. Words can point to God, but they cannot contain God. Creeds tell true stories of faith, but creeds can never exhaust the ongoing stories. God is beyond and more than any human system of thought. Countless times we have fallen into heresy by forging our small and partial truths into religious clubs to beat into submission anyone who did not agree—and always in the name of God.

There are those who seem to be convinced that God is a member of their worship tradition. God is not a Baptist, Episcopalian, Pentecostal, Presbyterian, Roman Catholic, Methodist, or any of the other varieties of religion that are part of this nation's religious heritage. God does not prefer the King James Bible or the Book of Common Prayer. The Episcopal Church, the King James Bible, and the Book of Common Prayer, we trust, all participate in and point to who God is, but God cannot be adequately described by those human constructions.

No nation or race captures the whole truth of God. God is not American, Russian, English, or Chinese. God is not white, black, or oriental. God is not a he. Yet each of these ways of describing God does share in the divine truth. We are simply limited by language, imagination, and finitude.

No faith system can claim identity with God. God is not a Christian, a Jew, a Moslem, a Hindu, or a Buddhist. Until we accept the partiality of all religious systems, our religious arrogance will violate God's word against bearing false witness. Allowing ourselves to know and feel the angst of uncertainty banishes us from the delusional comforts of home and sets us on the journey of faith.

Christians are not settlers, but pilgrims. Settlers circle their wagons and prepare to guard their turf against the enemy. But as pilgrims, Christians are always moving, always widening the circle of experience to gather new acquaintances who tell God-bearing tales of lives lived differently from their own. Unchanging conviction stops pilgrims in their tracks and puts an end to storytelling and therefore an end to living faith. "The passion for truth," wrote Paul Tillich, "is silenced by answers which have the weight of undisputed authority."

Christians are not museum curators who preserve the treasures of yesterday. We worship a tent God who is always ready to pick up stakes and move on, a God who is not overly fond of palaces and temples, creeds and doctrines, formulas and litanies.

How weary the holy God must be of our shallow ecclesiastical clichés! How the divine patience must be tested by our posturings, grandiose claims, and attempts to regulate our lives with a common vision and plan imposed on everyone!

Fallibility is part of the human condition. In our search for truth, the best we can hope for is a growing capacity to find wisdom in contradiction, truth in paradox. The capacity begins with the honesty to see ourselves as both wise and foolish, good and evil, strong and weak, believing and doubting, loving and uncaring. The broadening of self makes room for truth as it is, not as we wish it to be, so that we can say with Walt Whitman, "I contradict myself, I am large, I contain multitudes."

Opportunities for expanding awareness of our own personality come with age. As a young priest I identified with the groom at every wedding. As I grew older, with daughters reaching marriageable age, I suddenly realized that I looked at weddings through the eyes of the father of the bride, a very different perspective. I never will know the perspective or feelings of a bride or her mother or of a parent of a groom. All of those experiences are hearsay, even though I believe those who share them with me.

There is nothing objective about experience. The minute we think there is, we are in jeopardy of breaking the ninth commandment.

"You shall not bear false witness" is a call to escape the ignorance that plagues and distorts all human beings. It is a call to a new awareness, a new sensitivity. It is a call to come out of the dishonesty of our killing prejudices and the blindness that mistakes partial truth for ultimate truth.

"Know thyself" is ancient wisdom. Know thy limitations. Know thy finitude. In Shakespeare's play *Hamlet,* Polonius says to Laertes, "This above all: to thine own self be true; / And it must follow, as the night the day, / Thou canst not then be false to any man." When we accept ourselves, the need to bear false witness will fade, and the vicious, self-serving attacks of our human tongues upon our neighbors will cease.

Chapter 13

DESIRE AND ENVY

"He who withdraws from activities, but ponders on their pleasures in his heart, he is under a delusion and is a false follower of the path."
                                                              —BHAGAVAD GITA

The king stood at a window of the palace, pouting. He was staring at a vineyard that abutted the palace wall. For many days he had noticed how the sunlight on this side of the palace was just right for the garden he had long wanted to plant there so that the best and freshest vegetables could be cultivated for his table. The vineyard, however, belonged to another. It was a part of the land that had been in the family of Naboth of Jezreel for generations. The king had gone to Naboth and offered to buy the land for a fair price or to exchange another vineyard for this one. What difference would it have made? he mused. Is not one vineyard like another? That part of Samaria was laden with vineyards. But Naboth had obstinately refused the royal offer. He would not even discuss giving up his inherited land. Nothing more could be done. The divine law regarding sacred family land was clear for kings and farmers alike in Israel. With a great sigh, King Ahab flung himself on his bed, turned his face to the wall, and refused to eat or to join the others at table.

His haughty queen, noticing his absence, went into the bedroom to inquire about what was wrong. When she had heard the story, Jezebel was incredulous. "Are you the king or not?" she demanded to know. Her father, the king of Tyre in neighboring Phoenicia, certainly knew how to act like a king, with all the privilege that came with the title. "Get up, put a smile on your face, and eat," said the woman who was born to have her own way. "I will take care of everything" (1 Kings 21).

At this point Ahab and Jezebel began a rapid descent into the depths of evil. The word for "covet" in this tenth commandment, *hamad,* means "lay plan to take" or "have in mind to do a certain thing." In its original form, the commandment prohibiting coveting referred not to secret desire or wish for another's belongings, but to envy accompanied by a plan for action. It was the activity that brought one to the brink of theft that was sinful, not the isolated wish. As the story continued, Ahab's and Jezebel's plans for theft led them into further depravity that compounded their evil.

Jezebel left Ahab to his meal and set about her mischief. She wrote letters in Ahab's name with instructions for the magistrates who governed the sector of the city where Naboth lived. The letters directed them to find two scoundrels who would publicly accuse Naboth of cursing God and the king. This violation of the third commandment was punishable by death, so the law required that the witnesses be willing to be the executioners if their testimony brought about the death sentence. The wicked deed was done; Naboth was stoned to death outside the city wall, and Ahab quickly commandeered the vineyard for his own pleasure.

Ahab was king of Israel, however, and Israel, unlike Phoenicia, saw even kings as under the ultimate reign of an ethical deity. Elijah, the prophet of this holy God, found out about the dastardly deed and confronted Ahab and Jezebel. They heard God's judgment pronounced on them. Both Ahab and Jezebel met painful deaths—one in battle, the other in a palace revolt. The popular wisdom was that Elijah's words of condemnation had been carried out by no less than God. In one fell swoop, this royal pair and their cohorts had broken the law on five counts: coveting, stealing, murder, false witness, and, as we shall see, idolatry.

The tenth commandment was unlike any of the other nine, for it focused on the *intention* to wrong action. The others were concerned with the final outcome rather than with motivation. Scholars have had difficulty in reconciling the apparent anomaly. In order to locate the stealing of property under this tenth rubric, some attempted to restrict the eighth commandment to a prohibition against the stealing of persons, thus giving the tenth commandment an equally specific and overt content. They argued that the ordered life of the community was threatened only when malicious envy led to a plan that was then executed. However, the linguistic and historical evidence did not support such a thesis. Stealing was stealing. Coveting had to be different. Furthermore, when malicious envy moves to the stage of making plans, actions are taken. There are letters to write and witnesses to bribe. The preparation for evil is as damning as the evil itself. As we see in the Ahab-Jezebel story, the setting of the stage for Naboth's murder jeopardized the lives of the king, the queen, and their accomplices. All became subject to death through their conspiracy to murder.

The more serious implications of the sin of malicious envy are found in its connections with the commandment "You shall have no other Gods before me." In a sense "You shall not covet" is the behavioral application of that injunction. Jealousy is mine, says the Lord God. When jealousy is claimed by human beings, life is immediately distorted.

While the social prohibitions against murder, stealing, illicit sex, and lying under oath are found in nearly all ancient law codes, the first four commandments, which express the nature of God, are unique to the covenant people among their contemporaries. Surrounded by other cultures holding diverse values and worship traditions, the covenant people were tempted by their serious envy of other lifestyles, and so their communal life was marked with frequent backslidings. The mysterious ecstasies of the nature religions were seductive. Ridding the tents of idols and talismans and settling down to a sabbath regimen were not easily accomplished. From time to time the whole community was guilty of the kind of envy that fastened on the belief that the oasis was greener on the neighbor's side of the desert. The episode of the golden calf was an envious grasping for other gods, and the plan to appropriate another's religion was enacted in the making of the idol.

As the law was refined with the passing of time, more sophisticated and interior interpretations were applied. The prohibition came to be less concerned with the plans for theft. It focused more on the orientation of the mind and the recognized power of the contents of human thought to shape character. Increasingly this became the subject of the law's commentary. Here we begin to contemplate the genesis of human motivation, the birth spirit of influence that stirs the "evil imagination of the heart" as well as the poignant longings for love and being.

The issues of life are found in the mysterious, unknowable, un-manageable heart, the passionate beating pulse, the jealous (read zealous), single-hearted, faithful devotion to living and not dying, to becoming and not diminishing, to loving and not fearing.

The commandment against coveting moves away from overt con-scious actions and rivets our attention on those inner hidden and silent attitudes of our lives. The other commandments, at least until Jesus reinterpreted them in the Sermon on the Mount, focused on the external layers of human life as a camera focuses on the landscape. But commandment number ten focused on the internal self. It was a penetrating x-ray of the human heart. To experience the power of this commandment to judge required courage, for one cannot know the truth of this sin without a painful self-examination of the psyche. Since we would rather not believe the evil truth of our motivations, only the person who seeks the spiritual "path of the heart," as Carlos Castaneda's Don Juan names it, will carefully look at coveting and admit culpability. Most of us will simply ignore our will to possess, to succeed, and to be admired at the expense of our neighbor. Such evil imaginations are, after all, not subject to civil punishment, and no one will know, we reason. But the human heart is not so devious or so hidden as we would like to believe.

This commandment quite simply calls us to confess that we are not God. It extends the commandment forbidding idol worship by reveal-ing the result of putting the one who is filled with a covetous desire for person or thing into the place of God. When we are in the clutches of a "must have" feeling, logic and decency are closed out. It is as if some alien entity has entered us to lure us into believing that we alone know what will bring happiness and satisfaction.

Ahab's sulking behavior when denied his wish was not just child-ish; it was the behavior of someone who had lost all reason, who was possessed by a single thought to the exclusion of all others. This is the portrait of a man who was "beside himself" with envy and frustra-tion. Ahab's covetousness was not idolatry in the sense that the vineyard cum vegetable garden was imbued with holy qualities worthy of worship, for once owned it probably passed from his mind. Covetousness became idolatry rather when the king believed that he could fashion his world to his own liking, that he could determine what his needs were and thus organize the world for his benefit.

Covetousness is a lack of trust that God will be God, that God is the provider of what is finally necessary for life. It is an unwillingness to put oneself into the stream of the spirit where every event effects every other event in some ineffable way and where there are life-giving surprises that one could never anticipate, let alone desire for oneself. Coveting also seems to have consequences a bit hidden, but nonetheless overt and real.

The more we learn about consciousness and mental activity, the more respect we come to have for this prohibition against malevolent thoughts. It is here that religion and magic, prayer and spell are entwined in a Gordian knot. When the Western mind put its trust in reason and adopted a cause-and-effect model of reality, it discounted those common and uncommon experiences that fell outside these conceptual patterns. Such experiences were labeled paranormal or even psychotic. People who claimed to have passed through the inhibiting barriers of time and space in some mental fashion were dismissed as charlatans or treated as mentally ill. The religious discipline of prayer was devalued as a superstitious waste of time.

Since the turn of the half century, however, the rational cause-and-effect model has undergone serious questioning. Rapid transportation and instant communications have brought the Western mind into contact with people whose approach to life is very different. Our unbelieving eyes have had to grapple with amazing data that do not compute in the Western mind. For example, yogis can occupy cramped spaces for long periods of time. They emerge without ill effect even though measuring devices indicate that oxygen should have been depleted and muscles should have shown atrophy days before. Patients in China submit to major surgery without chemical anesthetic. Acupuncture as therapy does not fit into our medical model, but it works. Incontrovertibly, the mind appears to have the capacity to "know" far more than the conscious intellect can grasp.

The Swiss psychologist Carl Jung was an early modern proponent of the power of human thought. "I simply believe that some part of the human self or soul is not subject to the laws of time or space," he wrote. This conclusion set him on a course that moved toward therapy as self-healing. Prominent among his therapeutic tools was a mental activity he called "active imagination," the self-conscious imagining of a picture or story that the patient wants to come about. This intentional fantasizing can retreat into the past to heal old memories. It can enter the future by inclining the self in a particular direction. It can affect the present by creating the mental image of change here and now.

Mind cannot easily be reduced to mere brain activity. Mind suffuses the body and is so coupled with the body that their influence is mutual. Our mental and physical states of health are inseparable. Concepts of mind and soul are interchangeable; both are the source of thought, and both somehow hold the essence of personality. Whether the mind-soul can exist apart from matter has yet to be resolved. Theories of immortality and doctrines of God that propose a transcendent deity who exists apart from matter give an unqualified yes to the idea of a discarnate mind-soul. The Hebrew mind, however, rejected any thought of mind-soul separate from matter; hopes for eternal life among Jewish people were conceptualized in a future resurrected body. Current scientific theories of energy and matter speculate about the translation of mind-soul from one form of matter to another, as if the mind were software that could be played on various computer terminals. If these secular theories are sustained by continued research, then resurrection of the body and immortality of the soul become only different images of the same reality: the ongoing life of the mind-soul, a survival after the death of the product of the brain in some other system or mechanism.

Inquiries into life after death are far afield from the topic at hand and are worthy of their own separate treatment, but this excursion reinforces the idea of the mind-soul as having properties that are not bound by time and space and that may or may not be bound by its affinity for matter. The mind can transcend the limits of the body and do what the body cannot do. Through imagination the mind can travel through time and cross wide distances in an instant, moving faster than the speed of light. Yet to do this, the mind uses the physiological mechanism of the brain. But does thought have the power to make observable changes? Can we, through our thought alone, consult with the thought of other minds? If so, do inanimate objects and forces have anything that would correspond even in an ambiguous way with what we call mind in human life? If we were even to entertain that possibility, we would have to reopen our critical notebooks and rethink our intellectual abandonment of "miracle" and our sophisticated biblical interpretations of the apparently supernatural event as simply allegory, fable, or post-resurrection apprehension, told to illustrate a "greater" truth. If our assumptions about what is or is not possible in the physical world are discovered to be founded in false principles of natural laws, then not only we will have to rethink what Jesus of Nazareth might have done, but equally to the point, we will have to reevaluate our own capabilities as kinetic mind bearers.

The fact is, human beings are not power-less; we are power-full, far more than we will admit. We do imagine our way into our own futures. What we truly cannot imagine is not likely to happen. Only about ten percent of our minds is available to consciousness. The other ninety percent is hidden in darkness, undeveloped, forgotten, in the chaos of the "not yet." That unconscious mind contains most of our future as well as our past. Access to that undifferentiated potential creativity comes through altered states of consciousness: dreaming, trances, focused concentration and meditation, and, under carefully controlled circumstances, the use of certain drugs. The great burst of spirituality that has electrified the consciousness of countless people in the last two decades has emphasized disciplines of mental retrieval and consciousness raising. Meditation, yoga, body work, nutrition, and sensory awareness have done much to heal the dualist mind-body split and to bring more of our life force into our dynamic self-conscious existence. Such activities expand us both vertically and horizontally. They also unify the scattered and hidden components of our life into a single flowing consciousness.

The point is that our thoughts change us, and likely others as well. Our thoughts shape our characters and mold our bodies. As many have noted and one author used as a book title, *Ideas Have Consequences*. People who habitually think self-deprecating, trivial, condemning thoughts reveal those thoughts through their bodies as well as their words. We know the sad sack by his bent shoulders and collapsed torso. We know the trivial woman by her vacuous look and purposeless stance. We know the one who condemns by the invisible armor, the rigidity of body that covers vulnerability and prevents access. Thoughts, words, and deeds are not separate activities; they are different forms of a single attitude. Thoughts and images, every bit as much as words and deeds, have the power to bless and to curse, to heal and to wound. The ancient Hebrew injunction against coveting makes us aware that the first victim is one's own self.

Coveting understood as evil thought changes the self by its power to absorb attention and to damn one's own body and soul. The neighbor always knows in some way that the coveter does not love him or her. There is very little about our feelings for one another that we are in the last analysis able to conceal.

Given the current explorations into the character of mental processes, we want to leave open the possibility that evil thought might also have some direct malevolent result on the target of those thoughts. Our primitive ancestors would certainly have thought so.

It is insufficient to say that it is what we do and not what we think that matters. Though we can act our way into new ways of thinking, the reverse is also quite often the case. Our imaginations, thoughts, and desires are powerful forces for change in our lives. Wishes do come true, and prayers are answered. Perhaps someday we will understand the connection with its object. Suffice it now simply to issue the warning that we do need to be wary about what we pray for, wish for, hope for, desire, and imagine. It has an uncanny way of happening.

Wishes fulfilled are not, either in life or in our fables, always the boon we imagine. Often the recipient of the free gift from the genie, the changeling, the enchanted prince, or the fairy godmother is misused, or else greed oversteps what might have been a joyful opportunity.

Aesop, the moralist storyteller of ancient Greece, told of the honey bee who flew to heaven to give a sample of her honey to Jupiter. The god was so delighted that he promised to grant her any wish she desired.

"O great Jupiter, my creator and my master, I beg of you, give me, your servant, a sting so that when anyone approaches my hive to take the honey, I may kill him on the spot."

Jupiter was angered by the bloodthirsty request and granted the favor for the fatal sting, but decreed that the sting was to be fatal to the bee as well as to the invader.

Aesop's moral: He who prays hard against his neighbor brings a curse upon himself.

The familiar folktale recounted by the brothers Grimm illustrates how greed and envy feed on themselves and escalate into a confusion of the human self with the divine self, with unhappy consequences:

Once there was a poor fisherman who caught a wondrous fish. The fish pleaded for his life by explaining that he was really an enchanted prince. The fisherman acquisced to his request and spared him by throwing him back into the sea. When the fisherman related the strange happening to his wife, she, knowing the ways of enchantment, berated her husband for not bargaining for wealth in exchange for the enchanted prince's life. She sent her husband back to the fish to ask if they could have their lot in life improved. The fisherman reluctantly returned to the seaside and said:

> Flounder, flounder in the sea,
> Come, I pray thee, here to me;
> For my wife, good Ilsabil,
> Wills not as I'd have her will.

The fish returned and, when reminded of the debt he owed the man, granted the fisherman's wish for a new house. When the man returned to his home, he found his wife sitting on a bench before the door of a lovely new cottage. However, she soon became discontented and sent her husband back to request that the cottage be transformed into a castle. With a heavy heart he did her bidding, and her heightened wish was also granted. Not content with even those elegant accommodations, she began to think about her own position in life. She first asked to be king, then emperor, and finally pope. Each wish in turn was granted. As nothing seemed impossible, she sent the fisherman back one final time to make her last request. Now she wanted to be God, the Lord of heaven and earth.

Responding to the now-familiar rhyme from the seawall, the fish/prince asked what the woman wanted this time. Her terrified husband replied, "Alas, she wants to be like unto God." And with that the fish sent him home to his wife, who now sat in the hovel she had occupied when the tale began. "And there they are living to this day." So ends Grimm's tale.

The story does not give a clue about what it would be like to live like God. Clearly the woman's expectations were that God would live in a manner more pretentious and grand than any human had yet ever dreamed of living. The Bible's claim that God identifies with the humble, the poor, and the lowly causes one to wonder if the fish/prince did not grant the final wish after all.

Covetousness, a spiritual malady, leads us into the idolatry of self-designated divinity. Human beings are as inadequate representations of the One God as the carved stones of ancient peoples or the thought forms of those who would pretend to be privy to the secrets of truth. We live within the mind of God, in the give-and-take of the perpetually moving spirit whose jealous love will brook no other, who is less interested in what we know than in who we are.

The first and last commandments are like matching bookends that hold the center in place. Together they order and define the essential divine-human character. To obey the tenth and concluding commandment is to know that God is creator and we are creatures yearning to reflect that creator, but never usurping the creator's place. It is to be aware of the oneness of God and to see ourselves, one another, and all created things as part of that oneness. It is to live in harmony with life, opening ourselves to the awe and mystery that is all around us and that calls us into a mystical communion with God, with others, with ourselves, and with all that is. It is to allow the spirit-filled universe, carried by something like life-giving love, to surround us and to cause a constant birth of consciousness to occur within us. It is to live in the experience of self-acceptance that enables us to recognize the love that makes us capable of an answering self-love. It is to replace the envy for power or affirmation with the desire to be ourselves—our deepest, freest, truest selves, through which God's power might be seen. It was Irenaeus who observed, "The glory of God is a person fully alive." When we are lifted out of covetousness by the magnetic drawing power of the Holy God, we are whole and free and we become bearers of God, incarnations of the divine spirit, if you will.

So the commandments come full circle. The God who is one, requiring in the first injunction a single-minded worship, is now best seen when the worshiping creature, eschewing covetousness—the disease of a fragmented heart—lives out that divine oneness and desires nothing less in his or her life than to reflect the oneness of God, who is the source and sum of all things.

Chapter 14

POSTSCRIPT: COVENANT PEOPLE

"To go alone into the mountain and come back as an ambassador to the world has ever been the method of humanity's best friends."

—EVELYN UNDERHILL

Our discussion of the Ten Commandments is now complete. The book of Exodus moves beyond these holy words to record the balance of the Jewish law. The drama of the mountain encounter diminishes as the minutiae of Jewish cultic practice are described in intimate detail, filling not only the balance of the book of Exodus, but also Numbers, Leviticus, and Deuteronomy. This part of Israel's sacred history contains very few additional narratives. The one yet to be related is the familiar account of Moses' return trip to the mountain of God. Becoming anxious when Moses was delayed, the people prevailed upon Aaron to construct a golden calf for them to worship. They feared being alone in that inhospitable wilderness without divine protection. Aaron complied, setting the stage for a dramatic confrontation between, on the one hand, Moses and his God Yahweh and, on the other hand, the people and their superstitious religious fears. When Moses returned he saw the people's idolatry and in a fit of anger smashed the two tablets of stone on which the Ten Commandments presumably had been written. This episode added a provocative note to the portrait of Israel's primary founding father.

Under the influence of the royalist tradition of the southern kingdom, the sacred narrative constantly presented Moses in heroic terms. In these stories God spoke directly through Moses to God's people. Moses was the divine mediator, the larger-than-life-size figure to whom alone God talked face to face. This was not a budding democracy that the authors were describing; it was rather a hierarchical rule by divine election. God's pillar of cloud was said to have rested upon Moses' tent each day. As the chosen of God, Moses had enormous power. Moses alone could have dared to smash the sacred tablets, for only he could return to the mountain to have God write in stone once more the requirements of the law for the people of the covenant. In a secondary way, this episode also allowed the author to explain why it was that more than one version of the Ten Commandments appeared in the Torah.

The story of Exodus closes with the people of Israel busily engaged in the task of building a proper sanctuary for God. It was a portable sanctuary, for they were still a pilgrim people, destined to wander for an entire generation as nomads in the wilderness, learning, worshiping, preparing for the day when they would claim the land of the promise as their own land forever. The portable sanctuary indicated that the holy God could not be located in one place or contained in any human structure, not even in human words. God's word was always heard in the moving events of history. In our own complex twentieth century, worshipers of this same God are still aware that God is not confined by space or time. We are still eager to hear that word in fresh and relevant ways, for we continue to be a pilgrim people. The biblical text that we read as we travel is both a problem and a treasure. It is a text frozen in time, culturally and historically conditioned and filled with vocabulary and concepts of a world that is no longer. Yet beneath, beyond, and through that text the living truth of God can still be discerned. It continues to stretch and grow as new circumstances, undreamed of when the text was written, are nonetheless illumined by its words.

The Bible is called the word of God, but the words of the Bible cannot be *identified* with the words of God. That is a crucial distinction. The word of God is heard in the words of scripture; and wherever authentically spoken, it still gives life. When the word is lived out perfectly in history, as Christians believe it was in Jesus the Christ, then that incarnate word invites us into a life that death itself cannot extinguish.

Those who are bound together by that life-giving word are called the covenant people. The task of the covenant people is the same today as it was 3500 years ago. They enable the word of God to be heard again in every generation by interpreting it in the light of their particular moment in time. The newness of the moment gives a fresh vitality to the ancient words that continue to command allegiance and devotion. It is the covenant that unites us with the Hebrews who stood at the foot of Sinai. It is the covenant that inclines us to take their law and their commandments seriously, and to make them our own. New occasions do teach new duties, and time does make ancient good uncouth, but still the life of the covenant binds our journey to the journey of the people of God in every age.

Because we see ourselves as part of a historic company of covenant people, we have sought to lift the Ten Commandments out of antiquity and to interpret them for our day. We close this volume by attempting to describe what covenant people are like, that others might be called into this community.

Covenant people are people who risk. They are willing to step out of the known and into the unknown, there to live out stories that have unfamiliar and unpredictable plots. The covenant calls us to leave home, the comfortable and familiar place, to begin the journey by entering into an insecure world in the confidence that God always journeys with us. Nothing changes in life until we move, perhaps first in our minds, simply by imagining a different world and a different future.

To imagine change before it comes upon us is to take a leap of faith. The capacity to imagine is not always a welcome gift among those not willing to travel. Creative imagination brings discomfort and disappoints, angers, and offends those who do not see or anticipate or hope as the visionary does. Faith is never expressed as certainty, though it carries the weight of conviction. Faith is a feeling and a belief that gets translated into action. A life that has never interrupted a single cultural pattern is devoid of faith. The symbolic act of leaving home breaches the boundaries of the culturally accepted ways of thinking and acting. It unsettles common life, for it criticizes the present and opens the way into tomorrow for others to follow.

The courage to risk is contagious. One lone visionary can not only re-form his or her own life but can also be the first in an awakening that will re-form the larger group. It takes very few people to make significant changes, either for good or for ill. No wonder that in the name of preserving stability society abandons those who follow the quest for the unique self.

Those who voluntarily cast themselves outside the unthinking life of a culturally programmed myth are often considered abnormal; normal people, after all, are defined as well-adjusted. But normalcy can degenerate into thoughtless captive acceptance of the majority who parrot prepackaged truth. These "normal" people adjust to the compliant repetition of the inherited expectations. In time, such people become bored, depressed, joyless, passionless, and unenthusiastic (this latter a word whose root meaning is "unpossessed by God"). Socrates said that the unexamined life is not worth living. It might also be said that the unexamined life finally becomes one of self-annihilation.

As risk-takers, covenant people will always live in tension with the law in both its written and unwritten forms. They are not rebels who defiantly break the law. They are, rather, people who live through and beyond the law, for law is meant to contain and preserve; it permits order and peaceful coexistence. Law refers to the past for its validity, so when law is operating as custom, it inhibits the process that precedes new arrangements, stronger bondings, and different coalitions. Covenant people live at the edges of life. They journey into the theological and political wilderness. On occasion they give the appearance of being lawless, perhaps even immoral. Fresh truth almost always has the look of heresy; novelty is hardly ever orthodox. Covenant people are engaged in, or sympathetic to, such change-related activities as civil disobedience. They are willing to make personal, spiritual choices that risk general disapproval. Churches that give sanctuary to political refugees who are illegal aliens, couples who adopt interracial children, scientists who propose theories that can be neither measured nor observed, theologians who insist that God is not bound by traditional understandings of the supernatural—all are manifestations of those who live, think, and act in ways that subvert the values and beliefs of the dominant culture. But such deviations from the norm can also be the harbingers of a new consensus organized around new values.

The leading edges of the intellectual and moral breakthroughs are usually greeted at best with skepticism and apathy, and at worst with condemnation and punishment. Machiavelli observed in *The Prince,* "It must be remembered that there is nothing more difficult to plan, more doubtful of success, or more dangerous to manage than the creation of a new system. For the initiator has the enmity of all who would profit by the preservation of the old institutions and merely lukewarm defenders in those who would gain by the new ones."

When covenant people move beyond risk they tend to become stubborn. The journey is long and arduous, with periods of rest and occasional losses of nerve, but with no turning back or quitting. The re-visioning of a single life, let alone of an entire society, is a monumental and complex task. The world never seems to run out of dragons to slay, riddles to solve, or enchanted forests to explore. The temptation is always to retreat from the vision and to fall back into a deep sleep that ignores change where it can be ignored and resists it where it cannot be ignored. In Homer's *Odyssey,* the most dangerous time in Odysseus' journey was his stop in the Land of the Lotus Eaters, where life was easy and without cost or challenge. Knowing that he would never reach his destination if he succumbed to such narcotic and painless bliss, he left as quickly as possible. Risk begins the journey; commitment continues it.

Though they have no maps to tell us where we are going or how to travel, covenant people are surefooted because they remember where they have been. That process of remembering arranges random events and thoughts into a pattern that gives meaning to the present and thereby to the future. We live our lives forward, but we understand them backward. Remembering keeps us connected to the chain of persons and events that have formed, informed, reformed, and brought us to any given moment in time.

Not all change comes in the midst of turbulent and furious conflict. It also unfolds and develops out of the inexorable flow of time. The *I Ching,* a book of Oriental wisdom, states: "The movement is natural, arising spontaneously. For this reason the transformation of the old becomes easy. The old is discarded and the new is introduced. Both measures accord with time; therefore no harm results."

Remembering has a gentling effect on risk-taking, for it requires solitude, reflection, and attentiveness to the way things already are. Prophets and sages begin their anticipation of the future by attending to the present. The future cannot be forced. It can, however, be influenced by encouraging change in particular directions now. Covenant people are able to see into the eye of an eye and to feel the breath of a breath. They are able to let be in order to become; they do not resist or impede the divine will as it unfolds around and among them.

Lastly, covenant people are free and joyful because they are not alone. They journey as those who are bound together by an extraordinary love that is not negotiable. It is a love that is neither reasoned nor tepid. It is a love that sets on fire, an all-consuming devotion. One does not arrive at this state of passion by following a set of prescribed rules. To the people of Sinai, the courtship was in Egypt, the declaration of love was on the banks of the Sea of Reeds, and the law as given at the foot of the mountain was the way in which God and the people would live together now that they were passionately committed to one another.

As long as love lasts, the ties of love do not constrict. The bonds of fidelity keep love alive. They carry us over the arid times when we are empty of feeling and must wait until a renewal of spirit rekindles and revitalizes the relationship. Created in the image of their God, covenant people are lovers who bind themselves passionately to persons, institutions, ideas, and places. Like their God, they do not love abstractly but are faithful to love in the concrete and to earthly manifestations of life. Covenant people are willing to die for love: for some one, some thing, some where, some time. The passion of Christ and the passion of lovers are one, for to be passionately in love is to lose oneself in the arms of, or for the sake of, another.

"Blessed is the one whose delight is in the law of the Lord" (Psalm 1). Such a person is called to live fully, to love generously, even extravagantly, and in the community of the covenant people to be all that God created that person to be.

BIBLIOGRAPHY

Aesop. *Aesop's Fables*. New York: Grosset and Dunlap, 1947.

Alvarez, A. *The Savage God*. New York: Bantam Books, 1971.

Anderson, Bernard W. *Understanding the Old Testament*. Englewood Cliffs, N.J.: Prentice-Hall, 1975.

Bonhoeffer, Dietrich. *The Cost of Discipleship*. New York: Macmillan, 1972.

Bright, John. *A History of Israel*. Philadelphia: Westminster Press, 1972.

Buechner, Frederick. *Wishful Thinking: A Theological ABC*. New York: Harper & Row, 1973.

Capra, Fritjof. *The Turning Point*. New York: Bantam Books, 1983.

Childs, Brevard. *The Book of Exodus: A Critical Theological Commentary*. Philadelphia: Westminster Press, 1976.

Cirlot, Juan-Eduardo. *A Dictionary of Symbols*. New York: Philosophical Library, 1962.

Coward, Howard. *Pluralism*. Maryknoll, N.Y.: Orbis, 1985.

Dillard, Annie. *Holy the Firm*. New York: Harber & Row, 1977.

Fletcher, Joseph. *Moral Responsibility*. Philadelphia: Westminster Press, 1967.

Freud, Sigmund. *Totem and Taboo*. New York: Vintage Press, 1946.

Greeley, Andrew M. *The Sinai Myth*. Garden City, N.Y.: Doubleday, 1972.

Grimm, Jacob and Wilhelm. *Grimm's Fairy Tales*. New York: Pantheon Books, 1944.

Harrelson, Walter. *The Ten Commandments and Human Rights*. Philadelphia: Fortress Press, 1980.

Keen, Sam. *The Passionate Life: Stages of Loving*. San Francisco: Harper & Row, 1983.

Keen, Sam. *"The Faces of the Enemy."* San Francisco: Harper & Row, 1986.

Kolbenschlag, Madonna. *Kiss Sleeping Beauty Good-Bye*. Garden City, N.Y.: Doubleday, 1979.

Maslow, Abraham H. *Motivation and Personality*. New York: Harber & Row, 1970.

News of the Universe: Poems by Twofold Consciousness. Edited and translated by Robert Bly. San Francisco: Sierra Club Books, 1980.

Niebuhr, H. Richard. *Radical Monotheism and Western Culture*. New York: Harper & Row, 1960.

Noth, Martin. *Exodus, a Commentary*. Translated by J. S. Bowden. Philadelphia: Westminster Press, 1962.

Nouwen, Henri J. *The Living Reminder: Service and Prayer in Memory of Jesus Christ*. New York: Seabury Press, 1977.

Otto, Rudolf. *The Idea of the Holy*. New York: Oxford University Press, 1973.

Owens, Virginia S. *And the Trees Clap Their Hands: Faith, Perception, and the New Physics*. Grand Rapids, Mich.: Eerdmans, 1983.

Pfeiffer, Robert H. *Introduction to the Old Testament*. New York: Harper, 1948.

Phillips, J. A. *Eve*. New York: Harper & Row, 1984.

Spong, John S. *Into the Whirlwind*. San Francisco: Harper & Row, 1983.

Tolstoy, Leo. *Anna Karenina*. Edited by Leonard J. Kent and Nina Berberova, translated by Constance Garnett. New York: Modern Library, 1965.

von Rad, Gerhard. *Old Testament Theology* (Volumes I and II). New York: Harper & Row, 1965.

Wiesel, Elie. *Souls on Fire*. New York: Vintage Press, 1973.

Womanspirit Rising: A Feminist Reader in Religion. Edited by Carol P. Christ and Judith Plaskow. New York: Harper & Row, 1979.

INDEX

DA